Susannah

M000111267

THE
GOSPEL-CENTERED LIFE
IN EXODUS
FOR STUDENTS

Kristen Hatton

Study Guide with Leader's Notes

New
Growth
Press

WWW.NEWGROWTHPRESS.COM

New Growth Press, Greensboro, NC 27404
www.newgrowthpress.com
Copyright © 2018 by Kristen Hatton

Scripture quotations are from the ESV® Bible (*The Holy Bible, English Standard Version®*), copyright © 2001 by Crossway Bibles, a publishing ministry of Good News Publishers. Used by permission. All rights reserved.

Cover Design: Faceout Books, faceoutstudio.com
Interior Typesetting and eBook: Lisa Parnell, lparnell.com

ISBN: 978-1-948130-06-6 (print)
ISBN: 978-1-948130-07-3 (ebook)

Library of Congress Cataloging-in-Publication Data on File

Printed in the United States of America

25 24 23 22 21 20 19 18   1 2 3 4 5

Dear David and Jonathan,

May you always remember and rest in the faithful, loyal love
of the LORD, or as Dad would say, God's *hesed*.

CONTENTS

INTRODUCTION

WHY EXODUS?

When my daughter was in middle school I began a girls' Bible study for her and a group of her friends. Our group stayed together through their high school graduation, but I learned early on there were limited resources for students their age. I remember standing, staring at the teen section at my local Christian bookstore and feeling so discouraged and confused about what to teach. The offerings seemed limited to quick fixes for complicated teen issues—studies that missed dealing with the heart and applying the gospel—or feel-good messages for navigating a happy, successful teen life. I wanted something more. Teens needed more.

Teens need to have their eyes lifted off themselves to see the truth about who Jesus is. They need to be deeply rooted in his Word to learn who he is, and in more than a Sunday-school-answer way, why he is the answer to everything. They need to see his Word as the one unfolding story about Jesus. Otherwise the Bible doesn't make much sense, and it can seem more like disjointed bits of advice and rules. If this is it, no wonder it is read more with the goal of checking quiet time off the to-do list. Instead, teens need to see it as the daily "manna" needed for all of life.

I walked out of the bookstore empty-handed that day. I decided instead I would take a sermon series from my pastor-husband and rewrite it into a Bible study. And that's what I did with the books of John, Exodus, and Hebrews. I love all of those books, but my favorite study with my girls was in Exodus.

Seeing Jesus in the Old Testament was eye-opening for most in the group. It was exciting to discover Jesus in such unexpected places as the tenth plague, the wilderness, and the tabernacle. The Bible came alive in new ways and, I hope, changed the way they will always approach reading their Bibles.

This is my hope for other teens, too. The Bible is not intended to be an instruction manual or self-help guide from which to pluck verses that seem to fit our situations. From Genesis to Revelation, it is again the one story of Jesus. How we view and read our Bibles matters, and the more we read it in context, looking to see him, the more we will get the story straight about Jesus's perfect work and worth for us.

We see this in Exodus! In fact, Exodus lays out the pattern for redemption. The Israelites need a Redeemer. Throughout the book we see them grumble, complain, disobey,.worship false gods, and try to be their own Savior. It's pretty easy to see. What's not so apparent to us is how we are just like them. We, too, do all those same things. We, too, need a Redeemer.

But what we also see in Exodus is how God loves to give grace to the guilty. Over and over again he not only comes to the rescue of the Israelites, but he seeks to be in a relationship with them. Their hope and the hope of all humanity, which is enslaved to the rule and reign of sin, rest on the faithfulness of God to fulfill his promises. And that he does. What Exodus points to through the deliverance of God's chosen people is later fulfilled in Christ.

God in his faithfulness sent Jesus to rescue, recreate, and restore. We have this guarantee by his Word—the same Word that revealed himself to Moses in the bush as the great I AM and later showed Moses his glory as he proclaimed to be "merciful and gracious, slow to anger, and abounding in steadfast love and faithfulness, keeping steadfast love for thousands, forgiving iniquity and transgression and sin but who will be no means clear the guilty" (Exodus 34:6–7).

Apart from teens hearing about who this God is in light of our true condition, they won't see their deep need for a Redeemer. Therefore, my hope for this study is to equip them with gospel glasses from which to view all of God's Word, and specifically to see how the Old Testament book of Exodus is all about God's redemption in Christ. With these lenses for seeing Jesus written across these pages, may they come to understand how the gospel informs and transforms all of life.

HOW THIS STUDY IS ORGANIZED

The Gospel-Centered Life in Exodus for Students contains twelve lessons written in chronological order. With forty chapters in Exodus, expounding on each of them fully was not possible for this book. Instead, some chapters are grouped together, or even skipped, because the big-picture goal is for participants to see Christ in Exodus through the captivity, wandering, and waiting of the Israelites' journey, and ultimately the Promised Land.

HOW TO USE THIS STUDY

This guide allows both leaders and participants to work through each lesson in a small group setting. Additional leader's notes for each lesson are found at the back of the book. The Scripture passages are not written out, so it is necessary for leaders and participants to have their Bible and a pen.

Each lesson includes the following sections:

1. Bible Conversation
2. Article
3. Discussion
4. Exercise
5. Wrap-Up and Prayer

To kick off the lesson, an icebreaker question related to the text may get participants thinking and talking. From there, Scripture is introduced and read. Following this initial Bible Conversation, the article expounds on the passage, or draws out a particular aspect of the passage to help the participants better understand the lesson as a whole. The discussion time then takes the main ideas of the lesson and brings them to the participants' hearts in more specific ways. The exercise portion varies from week to week, but the goal is to further personalize what has been taught in each lesson. Finally, the lesson concludes with prayer.

A suggested time allotment for each section is given to help the leader keep the group on track to complete the lesson in one hour's time. The lesson book serves as an easy-to-follow script. But leaders should become familiar with the Bible text, lesson, and leader's notes (located in the back of the book) prior to the group meeting.

Each participant should have a lesson book and something to write with. For several of the exercises, participants will be asked to write notes in the book. If some participants end up sharing books, or if they don't use the same book for each lesson, they may wish to write on notepaper instead.

In two cases, additional materials are recommended: Lesson 2 calls for a whiteboard or flip chart. Lesson 12 suggests that each participant hold a coin.

In most cases, no outside reading is given. But prior to lessons 3 and 10, participants are asked to read the Bible text ahead of time. This is simply because there is too much reading to cover within the one-hour time frame.

1

FORGETFUL OR FAITHFUL?

BIG IDEA

God never leaves us stranded. We are never left to face our circumstances, situations, or sin alone.

BIBLE CONVERSATION *20 minutes*

Tell about a time you felt forgotten or abandoned by God (maybe due to sickness or death, or troubles at home or school, or hurts in a relationship). What are some of the lies about God you have believed when you have felt forgotten?

Today you will read about the Israelites' enslavement under Pharaoh of Egypt, and the birth and early life of Moses. As we read, put yourself in the shoes of the Israelites and of Moses. **Exodus 1:8–22** is our first passage. Have someone read it out loud.

What differing emotions do you think the Israelites felt as slaves in Egypt, and why?

Let's continue reading with **Exodus 2:1–10**. (Have someone read this out loud.)

What might be some reasons the baby's mom decided to hide him?

Moses was raised as an Egyptian, but when he grew older and saw how the Hebrew slaves were treated, he became angry and murdered an Egyptian for beating one of his people. Then Moses fled to the country to escape Pharaoh's demand that he be killed. Now we pick back up in the reading with the last two verses: **Exodus 2:23–25.** (Have someone read out loud.)

Think about what these verses tell us about God. What do you like best about this description of God, and why is it so good to hear?

****

Though this is only a beginning glance at Moses, he will be with you for the rest of Exodus. For further insight, read the article "God Hears You." Read it out loud together, taking turns at the paragraph breaks.

Lesson

GOD HEARS YOU

5 minutes

What Tyler has faced in his relatively short sixteen years of life seems unfair. As a young boy he endured a tough battle against cancer that included lengthy hospital stays in a city far away from home. Even though he has been in remission for years, the lingering effects on his body have prevented him from playing the contact sports other boys enjoy. In many ways you could say he was robbed of the carefree childhood it seems he deserves.

Now once again Tyler has been forced into an adult world of responsibility and suffering he wasn't ready for. With the unexpected loss of his dad, Tyler is now the man of the house. His mom is back in the workplace, leaving him often responsible for driving his younger siblings to their activities and handling extra chores at home. It's hard to hear his friends complain about their stress when they have no idea what it's like to juggle everything on his plate.

Has God forgotten Tyler? Do you think Tyler feels like the Israelites did as slaves under Pharaoh's evil regime? We know from their groaning they felt betrayed by God. What happened to God's promise to their forefather Abram? They had expected to live happily in their own land, not as captives in a foreign place. Why was God not making good on his covenant to deliver them?

Have you felt like the Israelites—forgotten by God? Have you struggled to see how something in your life could possibly be "good"? Have you read his promises to be with you and to give you all things but only felt more confused? Has God's inaction led you to feel abandoned or disillusioned?

You are not alone. At times we all wonder where God is. Believe it or not, he hears you, and he has not left you alone! We know this to be true because of the verbs used at the end of the second chapter: *heard*, *remembered*, *saw*, and *knew*. Each of these verbs in the Bible's original language is a derivative of the word *yada*, which means "to know intimately or to be concerned about." In other words, these verses tell us that God took notice of his people's cries and remembered.

It is not that God had forgotten about his covenant with the Israelites and then, after 400 years, remembered he had left them in a foreign land. No, *remembering his covenant* means he is ready to act. Now is the time to make good on his promise.

Since the day of the very first sin, God had spoken of a Promised One who would rescue his people and make all things right again. The Israelites were captives in Egypt; they needed rescue from life in the wrong place under the wrong rule. But all of us are captives to sin. We, too, need a rescue—an even bigger rescue from sin's rule over us.

Like the Israelites, our hope comes from a rescuer God provides. Moses is a preview of the Rescuer to come, a picture we now see clearly. God did act by sending his Son—the Promised One—to snatch his people out of the grip of Satan's tyranny, sin's slavery, and the fear of death. God is not forgetful, but faithful to all his promises!

But there is another piece of the story for you to know! When Jesus was in the garden before he was crucified, the thought of being separated from his Father was so great that he cried out, "My Father, if it be possible, let this cup pass from me" (Matthew 26:39). As you know, the cup did not pass from him, and Jesus did go to the cross.

Did the Father not care or hear his cry? By no means! The Father saw Jesus's pain and knew intimately what he was going through. But remembering his promise is *why* the Father turned down his Son's prayer and allowed him to suffer in his life on earth and die horrifically on a cross!

Jesus's prayer was turned down so that God would answer yours! Jesus did everything necessary to permanently redeem all of God's people for all time. By his perfect life and atoning death, we are freed from sin's bondage and the consequence of death. We are fully embraced by the Father and guaranteed he will never leave us.

In Jesus, God hears your cry. He remembers his promise and sees your oppression. He knows your pain, and he *did* something about it by giving you Jesus. He is not forgetful, but faithful!

DISCUSSION *10 minutes*

What circumstances or situations keep you from believing God knows you intimately and is concerned about the details in your life?

When Jesus prayed to escape suffering, God answered no to that prayer for the greater purpose of redeeming his people. How does this speak into your trials, suffering, and unanswered prayers?

Like the Israelites we need rescuing, even though we don't always realize it. When we fail to see sin as more than just bad, outward behavior, we minimize the power and influence sin has over us. In fact, Jesus came so we would no longer have to be slaves to sin, held captive by its power over us. By freeing us from sin, he also frees us to look more deeply at how sin can affect our hearts and motives (cf. Romans 6:17–18).

Lesson

EXERCISE

WRONG RULER

15 minutes

In our exercise today, we will further explore our enslavement to sin and why it is so important that we be reoriented back to God's faithfulness. Let's read the exercise out loud and answer the questions together.

One way sin seeks to enslave us is by playing into our emotions and circumstances to convince us life should be better. We think we should be happier, have more, or deserve a different lot than what we've been dealt. Sometimes these thoughts are fueled by how we compare ourselves to other people. But only God can fill the hole in our souls, or emptiness, so whatever else we turn to for peace and happiness will never last. The more we try, the further we follow the wrong ruler deeper into sin, and the more disappointment, frustration, and emptiness will settle in our souls.

For a real-life look at the progression of living under the wrong ruler, read what pop star Madonna once said in a magazine interview. Have someone read it out loud. Then answer some of the questions below.

> All of my will has always been to conquer some horrible feeling of inadequacy. I'm always struggling with that fear. I push past one spell of it and discover myself as a special human being and then I get to another stage and think I'm mediocre and uninteresting. And I find a way to get myself out of that. Again and again. My drive in life is from this horrible fear

of being mediocre. And that's always pushing me, pushing me. Because even though I've become Somebody, I still have to prove that Somebody. My struggle has never ended and it probably never will.[1]

1. What is enslaving Madonna?
2. What other examples of enslavement can you take from pop culture or the world around you? What things today can be particularly enslaving to teens?
3. In what ways does sin seek to enslave *you*? Think about what consumes your thoughts, what drives your worries, or what gives you fears similar to those the Israelites felt in Egypt. What comes to mind?
4. What about an insatiable hunger for acceptance, approval, and love from others? How is that enslaving? In what ways do you seek these things?
5. Because Madonna felt she was only mediocre, she had to keep trying to prove herself. When do you feel less than or empty from living under the wrong ruler? How do you try to find relief?

WRAP-UP AND PRAYER *5 minutes*

After looking at the exercise, you should be more tuned in to the sneakiness of sin. You don't have to be living in outright rebellion to be under sin's power and control. But the good news is that at the cross Jesus defeated sin and Satan once and for all. So when you are in Jesus, you have been redeemed by grace because you have faith in him. God views you as perfect because of Jesus's faithfulness in living the perfect life.

This does not mean you can go ahead and sin. It means God does not hold your sin against you, and he works in you to help you resist sin. This grace, and the sight of who Jesus is for us, creates a desire in us to live obedient lives, not out of duty but from delight at his awesomeness.

---

1. Lynn Hirschberg, "The Misfit," *Vanity Fair*, April 1991, 167.

But when we continue to do those things we do not want to do, or we fall back into the same sin patterns, we are never without hope.

As part of your closing prayer time, pray that God would help you to remember his faithfulness always, even when it seems as if he is not acting or when you feel you don't deserve it.

Lesson

2

THE GREAT I AM

BIG IDEA

Christ is the great I AM who promises to be present with us always, and to be the one we can fully trust.

BIBLE CONVERSATION *20 minutes*

Imagine you are a new underclassman student council member. To your surprise, you have just been selected for a highly visible role at your school's big charity event. Before your name was announced for the position, the teacher built up last year's senior leader and the record-breaking event as a challenge to the new group to be equally successful, if not more so. As the new leader of the event and also new to student council, consider what thoughts are going through your head!

Now share a personal example of a time you felt unworthy or ill-equipped for something you were asked to do. What are some reasons we feel unworthy at times?

The last lesson mentioned how Moses fled to Midian after killing an Egyptian who beat a Hebrew. Today's passage picks up with Moses as a shepherd in Midian. Just as God heard the Israelites' cry for help and was ready to act, neither did God forget Moses (exiled away from his people). Despite Moses having taken the law into his own hands, God planned to use him to lead the Israelites out of captivity.

In this lesson you will read a long conversation between God and Moses. It is divided into four sections below. Each section includes Moses's response or question to what God tells him. As someone reads each passage aloud, write down Moses's response to God in that passage. (You might have someone write on a board for all to see.)

Exodus 3:1–11 Moses's response: _____

Exodus 3:12–22 Moses's response: _____

Exodus 4:1–9 Moses's response: _____

Exodus 4:10–17 Moses's response: _____

List several things you learn about God from how he answers Moses's concerns.

Why do you think God spoke about his faithfulness and his plan to be good to his people *first* (in chapter 3:5–9), before telling Moses he was sending him to Pharaoh?

✳ ✳ ✳ ✳

There is much to unpack in the dialogue between Moses and God, so move to today's article, "What's in a Name." Read it aloud together, taking turns at the paragraph breaks.

Lesson

ARTICLE

2

WHAT'S IN A NAME?

5 minutes

When introducing ourselves to people, we give them our names. But for people meeting us for the first time, our names don't reveal anything about who we are. On the other hand, when people who know us well hear our names, they will not only visualize what we look like and what our voices sound like, but also things about our character and personalities, and maybe our family backgrounds and shaping influences. They might recall past conversations and shared experiences, what we are passionate about and believe in, and even how we might respond to certain situations. They know who we are by our names because we have history together.

Well, God had a history with the Israelites, but roughly four hundred years had passed since Joseph died and the Israelites became enslaved. During this time, no new revelatory word came from God. So though they cried out to God for deliverance, we really don't know what their feelings were toward him, or even if the one true God is who they were crying out to. Because Moses asked for God's name and asked who he should say sent him, it seems neither he nor the people knew who God was. But in the burning bush, Moses began to see a picture of God's character as revealed by his name, and so do we.

Whenever the word LORD appears in small capital letters in the Old Testament, it stands for *Yahweh*, or YHWH as written in the Hebrew language without any vowels. It is the name God identifies himself with to Moses—a name so revered that the Jews would not even utter it. Instead they would say *Adonai* for "my Lord." But the Bible uses the word *Yahweh* more than six thousand times whereas the generic name for God, *Elohim* or *El*, appears only twenty-six hundred times.[1] This points to God's desire to be known not as an impersonal, uninvolved deity, but known intimately by his people—by name. The question for us, as it was for the Israelites, is what God wants us to know about him from the name *Yahweh*. We'll focus on three aspects of God's character made known by this name.

I AM EVER-PRESENT

Yahweh is God's covenant-keeping name. It means "I am" and comes from a derivative of the verb *haya*, meaning an active presence. So, when God tells Moses, "I AM WHO I AM" he is saying, "I will be actively involved and present with you." To be uninvolved would be contrary to God's very essence. It is not who he is. He is a God who has promised (in his earlier covenants made to Abraham) to be present with his people.[2] And throughout Exodus he will make his continual presence with the Israelites known.

I AM HOLY

Moses was tending to his flock when God called out to him from a bush. Can you imagine Moses's shock and confusion over first a voice coming out of a bush and secondly a bush that is on fire but not being consumed? Nothing about this scenario is normal, so when Moses was told to take off his sandals and not come near, his immediate response was also to hide his face. God didn't tell him to do that, but he instinctively knew he was in the presence of something great and also very threatening.

---

1. "From Adonai to Yahweh: A Glossary of God's Names," *The Bible Study*, accessed December 28, 2017, http://www.bibletopics.com/biblestudy/154.htm.
2. John H. Sailhamer, *The Pentateuch as Narrative* (Grand Rapids: Zondervan, 1992), 244.

Fire is like that, isn't it? If you've sat in front of a campfire, you know how easy it is to become mesmerized by dancing flames. But what happens if you've thrown paper into it? It quickly becomes engulfed. Fire is both beautiful to behold and dangerous to stand before. Just like God.

What should've been a wildfire sending Moses running for cover was contained to a single bush that was not even consumed. This is why Moses hid his face. And the fact that, like Moses, we can stand in the presence of a holy God and not be consumed is a mystery hinted at here in Exodus. Later, through the person and work of Jesus, we will come to see why a God so holy that no sin goes unpunished also welcomes us to his throne of grace.

I AM FAITHFUL

God's holiness will be a central theme as we go forward in Exodus. But let's first pull back the curtain on the Israelites' history to see what God had promised Moses's ancestor. In Genesis 15, God promised to make Abraham a great nation by giving him descendants (the Israelite people) as numerous as the stars of the sky with a land to call home. But God said right then that it would not come until after four hundred years of suffering in a foreign land! After that time, God said he would bring judgment on that foreign nation and bring the people out with great possessions (see Genesis 15:14). This is exactly what God now tells Moses in Exodus, with the Israelites taking the Egyptians' silver and gold as God's promised provision for them. God is always faithful, and his word never fails.

Through the one story of the Bible, we see God's faithfulness as a covenant-keeping God. We could devote an entire study to tracing his promises through to fulfillment. When God declares, "I AM WHO I AM" we learn that he is the same yesterday, today, and forever. He is still today—for us—who he was to Abraham, Isaac, and Jacob, and to Moses and the Israelites. His faithfulness to provide, protect, and fulfill his promises never ceases.

For the remainder of Exodus, God will proclaim more of the meaning of his name. But isn't it interesting that God appeared to Moses to establish a relationship and guarantee his presence prior to beginning his rescue mission? Like Moses, we will face situations and trials, insecurities and doubts. But in those times (and all the time), we can know God is actively present with us because of his character, revealed in his name.

DISCUSSION *10 minutes*

Why do you suspect learning about the characteristics accompanying God's name might change the way you relate to God?

In the last week (or month, or semester), what circumstances or reasons have caused you to doubt God's presence or question his faithfulness to you?

Think back to the opening discussion about feeling unworthy. There are some important tie-ins to Moses: he fled Egypt because he murdered a man, but then God chose him to lead his people out of captivity. What should this tell us about God when it comes to our sin and failure to measure up?

I Am vs. I AM WHO I AM

15 minutes

Remember how God answered all Moses's concerns:

- When Moses said, "I am not the man to go," God said, "I am with you."
- When Moses said, "I don't know who you are," God gave his name.
- When Moses said, "I won't be believed," God gave signs.
- When Moses said, "I am not a good speaker," God said, "I am your Creator and will guide your mouth."

Every *I am not* from Moses is met with God's *I AM*. Every *I can't* is met with God's *I can*. Every *I don't have* is answered with God's *I will provide*! God is everything Moses is not, and he gives Moses everything he needs. God did not call Moses because Moses was worthy. No, God promises to be with those who are unworthy and know they need him.

Reflect on a present circumstance (or a particularly hard past season) in which you can identify with how Moses felt ill-equipped, unprepared, and not good enough. What task, conversation, situation, or trial were/ are you facing?

In the table below or on a sheet of notepaper, fill in the first column with your hesitations, doubts, or struggles. If possible, start your statement with *I am*. In the second column, write a combating truth for how God answers that for you as the great I AM. If you are unsure, bring it to the group discussion following this exercise. An example (which might apply to you, too) is given.

I am vs.	I AM WHO I AM
I am . . . a failure and struggling with depression. My grades aren't high enough. I'm not skinny enough. I'm not popular enough. Where is God? He seems to not care because nothing is going my way.	I AM . . . with you. Even when you don't see me I am actively at work for you. It may not look like you think it should or be in your timing, but I will not leave you, and I will accomplish all that I've set out to do.
I am...	I AM...
I am...	I AM...
I am...	I AM...

If you're comfortable doing so, share some of what you've written with the group. If you wrote down something in the first *I am* column, but had a hard time filling in the second column about how God meets you there, ask the group to discuss what truths about God could go there.

WRAP-UP AND PRAYER *5 minutes*

Before we pray, make a note that you have some outside reading to do before next time. This won't usually happen, but since it is a long passage it would be hard to read and study all of it during our next lesson. **Please read Exodus 5 through 12:32 on your own and underline or make notes about what stands out to you.**

Today for your prayer time, praise God by thanking him for what it means to you that he is the great I AM. Also ask him to help you cling to who he is during specific situations when it's hard to believe he is with you.

Lesson

3

PLAGUED

BIG IDEA

God is all-powerful, over all things, and as merciful as he is just.

BIBLE CONVERSATION *20 minutes*

Hopefully, you had an opportunity to read Exodus 5 through 12:32. Please share what you underlined, or your thoughts while reading this passage. Or tell which of the plagues would have been your worst nightmare, and why.

Now you'll focus on a couple of key sections, starting with **Exodus 5:1–8**. (Have someone read this aloud.)

Living in a culture of many different gods, Pharaoh did not refute the existence of Moses's God, but he made clear there was no way he would obey him. For what reasons do you think Pharaoh refused to bow down to God?

At the end of chapter 5, Moses voices frustration at God for seeming not to hold up his end of the deal. Moses says, "O Lord, why have you done evil to this people? Why did you ever send me? For since I came to Pharaoh to speak in your name, he has done evil to this people, and you have not delivered your people at all" (vv. 22–23). Turn to **Exodus 7:1–5** to see how God responds. (Have someone read it.)

How does God's response challenge our understanding when we think he's done something that is not good?

* * * *

It's easy to read about something like the plagues or even current natural disasters in the news and not grasp the full extent of it because it doesn't personally affect us. But if you think about how bent out of shape we get over the loss of electricity or even a dead cell phone battery, it helps give a little perspective to just how bad each of these plagues would have been. The following article will explain further what the plagues mean. Read the article aloud, taking turns at the paragraph breaks.

WHAT THE PLAGUES REVEAL ABOUT THE ONE TRUE KING

5 minutes

Through Moses, God warned Pharaoh of the impending plague of hail by telling him,

> For this time I will send all my plagues on you yourself, and on your servants and your people, so that you may know that there is none like me in all the earth. For by now I could have put out my hand and struck you and your people with pestilence, and you would have been cut off from the earth. But for this purpose I have raised you up, to show you my power, so that my name may be proclaimed in all the earth. (Exodus 9:14–16)

Two thoughts jump out at me in this warning. One is that God had a purpose in placing an egotistical tyrant like Pharaoh in position of authority. The second is that God uses tragedy and suffering to accomplish his sovereign, holy, and perfect will. Both point to God's goodness to address the age-old question of why God allows bad things to happen—though we likely will still wrestle with this question for the remainder of our earthly lives. However, there is more here for us to learn about God.

At this point in history, there was no one greater than Pharaoh. He was the most powerful king of the most powerful nation in the world. No one would approach him with any request without much fear and trembling. You can imagine, then, the butterflies Moses and Aaron must have felt when telling him about each plague that came as a consequence of his refusal to let the Israelites go. You can probably also see why Pharaoh would be so obstinate. Again, in his mind no one had greater authority than he did. But no one is like God. And through Pharaoh, we see that anyone who thinks he is greater than God and has control over his own life is wrong.

Through the destruction brought upon Egypt, which neither Pharaoh nor his magicians or mighty men could do anything to stop, God showed Pharaoh who was really worthy of all praise and worship. And not just Pharaoh—God's display of power was also for the Israelites, Egyptians, and all people in all times to see who the one true God really is. God is the giver of every blessing found in this world, and also the one who removes these blessings or restores them as he wishes, for his glory.

God's glory is even seen through judgment. This is because, contrary to what we presume about judgment, his ultimate purpose is not to destroy; it's to save! When God warned about the plague of hail, "whoever feared the word of the LORD among the servants of Pharaoh hurried his slaves and his livestock into the houses, but whoever did not pay attention to the word of the LORD left his slaves and livestock in the field" (Exodus 9:20–21). God could have acted without giving a heads-up or any exceptions, but he chose to grant mercy to anyone (Israelite or Egyptian) who believed his word. So here in the plagues we see how God's plan for a chosen people has always included the whole world. His mercy in salvation is that all people who trust the Word—who is Jesus Christ—will live eternally with him.

Pharaoh didn't even have the control he thought he had over his own heart. The Bible at times says Pharaoh hardened his own heart and, in other places, says it was God who hardened Pharaoh's heart. Pharaoh's power and attitude against God was all part of God's sovereign will for his name to be proclaimed throughout all the earth. However, even Pharaoh received mercy and delayed judgment. God told him, "For by now I could have put out my hand and struck you and your people" (Exodus 9:15).

We will never understand why God has mercy on some and not others. But when we understand that we all deserve his wrath, the fact any of us receives grace becomes the bigger surprise. Like the Egyptians, we all turn to worthless, powerless false gods. Like Pharaoh we make a false god even out of ourselves, thinking we are in control and hold the power to our destiny. And yet God moves toward us with compassion, as he did when he heard the Israelites' cries.

Through the plagues, we see God's sovereign will, his power and authority over all, and his justice and mercy. This is a picture of what our sin deserves and the grace God gives through his Son. His Son took our deserved judgment and wrath from God so that we might be spared. His Son is God's mercy to us, even though we deserve what the Egyptians experienced in these plagues. He is the great I AM, the only true King worthy of worship and obedience.

DISCUSSION *10 minutes*

In reading about Pharaoh, what things could you say are true of someone with a hardened heart, and how do you see yourself at times acting as he did?

The idea of God's justice and wrath being paired with his goodness and grace is hard for all of us to understand. And even though this article shows us his mercy through his judgment, it is still a mystery why God chooses to be gracious to some and not others. But as we see more of our sin and rebellion against God, the real question becomes why me?

How do you think the plagues affected the Israelites' view of God and themselves?

When have you seen God's glory and goodness through his allowance for sin, suffering, or trials in someone's life? Have you seen God's goodness through your own trials?

WHO IS MY TRUE KING?

15 minutes

Like Moses, we might grow impatient and disillusioned when God does not act according to our own time line. We want to control our lives and think we know best. How is this like making your own self a false god?

Like Pharaoh, we want to reign supreme. To the right of the self-centered heart throne illustration below, or on a sheet of notepaper, list some areas and situations in your life where your heart has a tendency to be hardened to God and set only on self. For example you may realize, "*When I don't get invited to the party, I don't believe God is for me, and am jealous and rude to my friends who were.*"

Why is God taking all my friends from me?

Write out a prayer of confession and repentance for those things you've listed above. Ask God to help you have the eyes to see when you are struggling to be your own god and to keep you from a hardened heart.

_____

_____

_____

_____

_____

_____

_____

_____

_____

If you are willing, share some of what you wrote next to the heart.

If God is your true King, how by his grace might you respond differently to those areas in your life or circumstances where you have lived as if you are God?

WRAP-UP AND PRAYER *5 minutes*

Next time we will focus entirely on the tenth plague—the death of the firstborn—and what that means, along with the institution of the Passover. Let your closing prayer today include thanking God for his grace and mercy to you.

Lesson

4

THE TRUE SACRIFICE

BIG IDEA

God provides the lamb—the Lamb who is Jesus, our ultimate sacrifice.

BIBLE CONVERSATION *20 minutes*

Today's reading includes the institution of the first Passover, an Old Testament feast that is still one of the Jewish people's most important religious celebrations. Passover recalls God's faithfulness in delivering the Israelites out of Egypt. But before you get there, you will look specifically at the last plague—the death of the firstborn.

This lesson has several readings from Exodus 12 and 13. They are divided into sections for you. Have someone read each section aloud.

Exodus 12:1–6

Exodus 12:7–14

Exodus 12:29–36

What might be some reasons the Israelites were to be ready and eat the meal in haste?

What do you imagine it was like for the Israelites and the Egyptians the night all the firstborns, except those protected by the lamb's blood, were killed?

Continue your reading to see what further instructions God had for the Israelites.

Exodus 13:3–10

Exodus 13:11–16

If you were an Israelite father explaining to your children why you are having this feast, what would you want them to know?

How difficult do you think it would have been for the Israelites to set apart for sacrifice all firstborn animals, as well as one in the place of their firstborn sons? Why do you think God asked them to do so?

✳✳✳✳

These types of questions challenge us to think more deeply about the Scriptures. There is so much richness in all of God's Word, but the book of Exodus particularly mirrors our own story of redemption through Christ. To discover more about this, read aloud the article, "The Significance of the Firstborn," taking turns at the paragraph breaks.

Lesson

ARTICLE

THE SIGNIFICANCE OF THE FIRSTBORN

5 minutes

"Why do I have to be the oldest?" I can't tell you how many times my daughter has voiced some variation of this sentiment over the years. You may be the oldest and feel differently. But she and many firstborns feel as if they are their parents' guinea pig, or test run, as they work to figure things out. Many times, because of it, firstborns also feel they are held to a higher standard than subsequent siblings. Whether or not this is true, life for firstborns today is nothing like what it was in the Bible.

In ancient culture, the firstborn son received the family's birthright, which meant he carried the weight of his family's future. The family name and line continued through him, which is why the genealogy lists in the Bible are so important. Being firstborn also meant that upon the death or absence of the father, the firstborn son bore all rights and responsibilities to provide and protect. He also received double the inheritance of the other sons, because as the principal heir and firstfruit of the mother's womb, he was honored accordingly.

In our passage, the Israelites were told to set apart for God "all that first opens the womb," or firstfruits, to commemorate their exodus out of Egypt. This meant all firstborn animals were to be offered up as a sacrifice, and each firstborn son was to have a substitute sacrifice made in

33

his place. Because of the value and status placed on the firstborn, the Israelites were giving up their very best, an animal they would have viewed and treated as a pet. So this was a costly sacrifice for a ceremony with great significance.

We are told in Exodus 13:14 that in time the Israelite sons will ask their fathers what these sacrifices mean. And the fathers will tell them about the LORD who redeemed them out of the land of Pharaoh. But along with the story of their deliverance would come the retelling of the plagues, including the killing of all firstborns in Egypt, which is what finally led Pharaoh to relinquish his authority over them.

Can you imagine hearing this as a boy? It would sound terrifying and confusing. And it *is* terrifying if we don't get the story straight. We must see not only the wrath, but also God's grace.

First, a warning went out to Pharaoh and to all the people about the coming tenth plague. There was only one way that any animal, Egyptian, or even Israelite was safe—the smearing of blood over the doorway of their house. God would know by this sign to pass over and spare those under its cover. This is grace. God made a way to escape the sentence of death. But without the blood, he would execute judgment.

To get the blood, a sacrifice had to be made. Some living thing would have to pay the price of death. This is what the Israelites and Jews, to this day, remember through the Passover celebration. But there is more to be told that we can't miss.

Fast-forward to the New Testament when Jesus came on the scene. Right before his death, he celebrated the Passover meal with his disciples. As the host at the meal, Jesus took the unleavened bread (sound familiar?) and broke it, saying, "This is my body."

The disciples did not yet understand that Jesus's body would literally be broken to pay the debt of sin for all of God's people. They didn't know that the one who presided over the meal featuring a sacrificial lamb was himself the promised Lamb of God.

"Behold, the Lamb of God, who takes away the sin of the world!" (John 1:29). John the Baptist spoke these words about Jesus in the New Testament, but they are what Exodus and the entire Old Testament reveal. Jesus, the only begotten, firstborn Son of God, is the unblemished Lamb, the one who came to be the perfect required sacrifice.

It is his blood we need to cover us. And he gave it to us when he went to the cross and bore all of God's judgment so God's wrath would pass over us. The maker of all things was unmade on the cross in order to remake us to be God's firstfruits—his children.[1]

Exodus 12 is our redemption story! In Christ, we have been given new life because God in his grace and mercy to us sacrificed his own prized possession, his Son.

DISCUSSION *10 minutes*

In what ways do the Passover lamb and the firstfruits offerings point to Jesus?

Why is it important we not dismiss or downplay God as Judge?

How does seeing God's justice carried out as it was in today's lesson shape your understanding of God's grace? How does undeservedly getting his grace and mercy make you feel?

---

1. Peter P. Hatton, "The Story of Redemption" (sermon, Redeemer Presbyterian Church, Edmond, OK, June 7, 2015).

THE LAMB OF GOD

15 minutes

Do today's exercise together as a group. Have each person in your group look up one or more of the passages and read them aloud in the order they appear in the list below. These readings, adapted from a liturgy created by Rev. Robert Charnin, extend from the beginning of the Bible in Genesis to its end in Revelation, showing how the lamb is God's provision for his people.[1]

After hearing each passage, decide which title from the list below best matches the lamb described, and write it next to the passage.

1 Genesis 3:6–7, 20–21 *the lamb who cover our shame.*

2 Genesis 22:1–2, 6–14 *the provided lamb*

3 Exodus 12:5–7, 13 *the passover lamb*

4 Leviticus 1:2–4 *the unblemished lamb*

5 Isaiah 53:5–7 *the lamb wounded for us*

6 John 1:29–30 *the coming lamb who removes sin*

---

1. Robert A. Charnin, "Lamb of God: Creating a Service Based on Lamb Passages in Scripture," *Reformed Worship*, December 2000, 3.

7 Acts 8:26–35 *the lamb who is Jesus*

8 1 Peter 1:18–19 *the ransoming lamb*

9 Revelation 5:6–10 *the reigning lamb*

- ~~The coming Lamb who removes sin~~
- The Lamb who is Jesus
- ~~The reigning Lamb~~
- ~~The Lamb who covers our shame~~
- ~~The provided Lamb~~
- The ransoming Lamb
- ~~The Passover Lamb~~
- ~~The Lamb wounded for us~~
- The unblemished Lamb

Before this exercise, had you ever seen or known how Christ could be traced throughout the entire Bible as the Lamb of God? What stands out to you about Jesus from this exercise?

WRAP-UP AND PRAYER *5 minutes*

Instead of prayer, for your wrap-up today you may choose to listen to the song "Behold the Lamb" by Keith and Kristyn Getty and Stuart Townend. Feel free to close your eyes or sing along.

You can find the song online at a video sharing site, or at this link: http://www.gettymusic.com/behold-the-lamb/

5

FREEDOM

BIG IDEA

God is the author and the finisher of our salvation, the only one who can deliver us from slavery and death to freedom and new life.

BIBLE CONVERSATION *20 minutes*

Think about your emotions and behavior when you are stressed, anxious, or fearful. These are symptoms of something deeper. If you trace them downward, what do you think is at the root underneath the stress, anxiety, or fear?

Last time, you read how Pharaoh let the Israelites leave Egypt and head to the Promised Land. In this lesson they will experience a big plot twist that brings tremendous fear. Even if the story of the Red Sea crossing is familiar to you, listen for new details as you read **Exodus 13:17—14:31** together. (Have someone read it out loud, or take turns.)

If you had been an Israelite watching Pharaoh's army coming, what do you think your response would have been?

Can you recall a time you struggled to trust God? Did you confess the struggle to him? Why might it be hard to admit you don't trust God or are angry at him?

In telling the Israelites to be still, or silent (14:14), what do you think God wanted them to learn about him and themselves?

****

The article will more fully address this question and help you see how God fights for you and delivers you. Read it aloud, taking turns at the paragraph breaks.

THE LORD WILL FIGHT FOR YOU

5 minutes

For four hundred years the Israelites labored as slaves under Pharaoh's regime. When he finally let them go, they didn't make it far before Pharaoh changed his mind, gathered his army, and pursued them. By the time the Israelites realized the army was coming up behind them, they were trapped. With mountains surrounding them, the sea in front of them, and the Egyptians closing in on them, there was nowhere to flee. Can you imagine their fear?

With no way out, death seemed certain. It's no wonder they lashed out at Moses. They could not see anything beyond their circumstances, so their fear took over and controlled them. It's the same way for us. Whatever we go through that causes us to fear (a loved one getting cancer, your parents divorcing, having to move, friends rejecting you—whatever it is) takes our emotions, decisions, and reactions captive.

When this happens, it's hard for us to see what's really true. Our bad circumstances seem more real to us than God's Word. We can't see the truth that God is good. We don't believe he cares for us, and we doubt he will make things better.

Since this happens to us, too, we understand how hopeless the Israelites must have felt. Don't you know that when Moses said, "Fear not, stand firm, and see the salvation of the LORD, which he will work for you today" (Exodus 14:13) the Israelites must have been standing there with their arms crossed and eyes rolled back in their heads? I imagine the sneers coming from under their breath were something like this: "We are about to die and you are telling us not to fear? Are you kidding right now, Moses?"

Can you relate? Even though most of us have not experienced a near-death encounter as the Israelites did, trusting God in the middle of much smaller and less significant circumstances is still hard. We say we believe, but our fear and anxiety say otherwise. We try to take control because we don't really believe God will act according to our good—just as the Israelites thought.

So leading the Israelites to a point of desperation was all part of God's plan to show them their need to trust him in all circumstances. They could do absolutely nothing to save themselves, and that is exactly what God wanted them to see. It is as if he said, "You just sit there and watch and I'm going to do it for you. And I'm going to do it in such a way that only I can." And then God went to work!

Can you imagine how big the Israelites' eyes must have become when they saw the sea part in two? Maybe they started to feel a twinge of hope. With the Egyptians still on their tail, they would have remained uncertain and nervous about how this was all going to work. But silently they stepped forward onto the dry ground of the sea.

Now, for a minute, picture yourself at a football game watching your favorite team. Your team has been trailing the whole game, but with less than one minute left on the clock, they score a touchdown to win the championship. Can you hear the crowd? One minute it is like one big collective breath being held; the next minute the roar in its place is deafening. This is how I imagine the change in the atmosphere when the waters the Israelites had just passed through engulfed the Egyptians.

"Wow! God did it!" All they could do was marvel at his power and might. Do you see what a picture this is for us?

The Red Sea story sets a pattern for God's deliverance of his children from darkness to light. The Israelites had wanted nothing to do with God after Moses's first talk with Pharaoh went badly, and yet God did everything necessary against impossible circumstances to bring them out of slavery and death and deliver them to freedom. This is just what God does for us, too. It's our redemption story!

We are helpless in our slavery to sin. We can't escape on our own—we don't even want to. And our false gods can't deliver us either. When we turn to our false gods, we are really just trying to control our own lives rather than be still and surrender that authority to God. Only God can change that desire; only he can remake a sinful heart set on self see its need for a Savior.

And because God does the impossible in accomplishing our salvation, why should we expect anything less than for him to carry us until completion? Romans 8:32 tells us, "He who did not spare his own Son but gave him up for us all, how will he not also with him graciously give us all things?"

God showed the Israelites that he alone can save. But the Red Sea also serves as a pivotal marker—a reminder—of who God is and why he is trustworthy. He made the Red Sea crossing an event the Israelites and their future generations would look back at to remember what God had done for them.

He gives us these markers, too. After we have experienced trials and look back on them, we can often see how God's hand was on us. May these serve to help us remember his faithfulness. But even more, by his grace, may we see that nothing is surer than his Word, ultimately given to us in the person of Christ. Jesus is our guarantee "the LORD will fight for you." He came so we could be delivered from death and risen to new life in him.

DISCUSSION *10 minutes*

We tend to think lacking faith and doubting God makes us bad Christians, but have you ever considered that even our ability to trust God comes from God? How does hearing this make you feel?

Weakness and helplessness sound like terrible attributes in our culture that prides itself on being strong and independent. How do we tend to live as if we were strong and able? Why is it important that we not do this?

How do you see the Red Sea crossing as a pattern for our salvation?

You can't swim away
from your sin.

Lesson

EXERCISE

REMEMBER THE RED SEA

15 minutes

Trusting God and being still are hard because we prefer to take control of our circumstances. But just as God went before and behind the Israelites to deliver them, he controls events for our good, too. So both the Red Sea account in the Bible and events in our own lives serve as markers to help us remember how God is for us.

For today's exercise, spend a few minutes answering each question on your own before you go through them together.

1. Write a few sentences about a situation or trial where you have seen God's faithfulness to you.

   my crippling depression,

2. How can remembering that experience and how God saved the Israelites at the Red Sea help you when you doubt God's goodness or feel like you are all alone?

I will not be ferced to swim away from my deppresson

3. Where do you need to see and know that God will fight for you right now?

everyuhere bitch

4. What would it look like for you to be still? How do you think being still would change your anxiety or fear?

(not moving) probebly

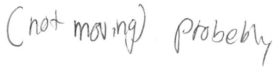

Share with the group some of your answers.

WRAP-UP AND PRAYER *5 minutes*

As part of your prayer time today, ask God to help you be still and know that he is God. Ask him to help you stop trying to control your life or save yourself, but rather trust him to be the author and finisher of your salvation.

Lesson

6

BREAD OF LIFE

BIG IDEA

Jesus is the true bread we need to sustain us for all of life.

BIBLE CONVERSATION *20 minutes*

Think about how you have felt toward God when he has not answered your prayers either in the way you wanted or in the timing you thought best. What did it take to warm your affections back toward God?

The Israelites also struggled with seeing God's goodness when he didn't provide for them as quickly as they wanted. Begin by reading **Exodus 15:22–27**. (Have someone read the verses out loud.)

At the end of the passage God says, "For I am the LORD, your healer" (v. 26). In what way is the Lord the healer for the Israelites, and for you?

God turned the bad water into drinkable, life-sustaining water. This is a theme that will continue as we move into our next passage, **Exodus 16:1–12**. (Have someone read the verses out loud.)

If you were to describe God's character, based on this passage, what would you say about him?

Let's continue reading with **Exodus 16:13–32**. (Have someone read the verses out loud.)

Verse 29 says, "The LORD has given you the Sabbath." How is the Sabbath a gift, in the same way manna was a gift?

****

For a clearer understanding of these Old Testament passages, we have the beauty of the New Testament. Today's article takes you to the book of John to shed more light on the true manna God provides. Read it aloud, taking turns at each new paragraph.

Lesson

ARTICLE

WHAT IS IT?

5 minutes

Most of us enjoy bread just fine—with a meal. But bread *as* our meal is probably not our preference. Certainly, bread for every meal, 365 days a year for 40 years, would not be our choice of food. Even our favorite food every day would start to get old! I think even my husband, who loves chips and queso more than anything else, would start grumbling long before day 14,600!

But God was intentional when he chose plain, ordinary bread to sustain the Israelites day after day. *Manna* in Hebrew means "What is it?" Not only did the Israelites not know what it was, they didn't see its significance. And without the New Testament we might miss seeing it, too.

Let's fast-forward to Jesus's earthly ministry. You may remember how Jesus miraculously multiplied a boy's five loaves of bread and two fish to feed the crowd of five thousand. Even after everyone was full, twelve baskets of bread were left. This sounds like the Israelites having extra manna to collect each day, more than enough even to eat on the Sabbath.

The next day the crowds found Jesus again, but he questioned what they were really seeking. Was it him they wanted, or only the benefits, such as endless food, that came from being with him?

The crowd responded by saying, "Our fathers ate the manna in the wilderness; as it is written, 'He gave them bread from heaven to eat'"

(John 6:31). In other words, "If you are really the Messiah, back up who you claim to be. As it stands, Moses is more impressive than you!"

Ouch! That sounds harsh, and for those of us who know Jesus is who he claimed to be, we think, *How foolish!* But without realizing it, we, too, want God to prove himself to us when it seems he's not providing as he should. Whether out loud or in our hearts, we say things like this:

- "If you really love me, God, answer my prayers the way I want!"
- "You don't care about me, God, because nothing ever goes my way."
- "You may be God, but right now you sure don't make me feel as good as that false god over there."

What's amazing is how God responds as Jesus did to the crowds that day—with grace. Jesus said, "Truly, truly, I say to you, it was not Moses who gave you the bread from heaven, but my Father gives you the true bread from heaven. For the bread of God is he who comes down from heaven and gives life to the world… I am the bread of life; whoever comes to me shall not hunger, and whoever believes in me shall never thirst" (John 6:32–35).

Light bulbs should be going off in your head if they haven't already. Here Jesus tells us plainly, "I am the bread." Not just any bread, but bread that sustains for life. Feed on Jesus and you will always be filled. Can you taste and see this is true?

After a while, the Israelites wanted more than manna. They grew tired of the bread, and it no longer satisfied their taste buds in the way it once had. Even the way it poured down out of the sky day after day became rather ordinary to them—not the miracle it first was. Likewise, for some in the crowd at Capernaum, there was nothing spectacular about Jesus. They knew him simply to be the son of Joseph the carpenter. They must have thought he was either a liar or lunatic (maybe both), but certainly not the Lord who had come down from heaven!

If we are honest, we realize we are no different. We too start to think Jesus is not enough. Even in our churches and student ministries, the gospel of Jesus Christ becomes overshadowed by what feels spectacular—the music, the lights, the games, the food, the *extras*. We may feel the same about time spent reading our Bibles; feasting on Jesus as *the* Word seems mundane. How much easier it is to get excited about experiencing Jesus at a concert, retreat, or camp. Those things seem to better capture the mountaintop high we try to bottle and hang on to.

But what a mistake this is—to gauge how our walk with God is going by our changing emotions! We don't need those new ways to "get on fire for God" or fix ourselves. No, we need the routine, regular Bread of Life. We need Jesus daily.

At the institution of the Lord's Supper, Jesus gave thanks and broke bread for his disciples to take and eat. When he gave them the bread he said, "This is my body, which is given for you, Do this in remembrance of me" (Luke 22:19). Then he took the cup after they had eaten and said, "This cup that is poured out for you is the new covenant in my blood" (v. 20).

Jesus has given us the bread (his body) and the cup (his blood) so we may always remember that through his life and death he is our perfect provider. In every way we fail to measure up and live the Christian life, he has already accomplished it for us. We look to him—nothing else—as our guarantee that the Father loves and accepts us. In Christ we lack nothing. He has given us everything we need for all time.

DISCUSSION *10 minutes*

How is the physical bread—the manna—in Exodus a pointer to the true bread? In other words, how does the manna function similarly to Jesus as the Bread of Life?

What does it mean that Jesus is enough, and why is it hard for you to trust he is?

Lamentations 3:22–24 says, "The steadfast love of the LORD never ceases; his mercies never come to an end; they are new every morning; great is your faithfulness. 'The LORD is my portion,' says my soul, 'therefore I will hope in him.'" Like God's faithful giving of the manna, these verses remind us that his giving of mercy and grace are also unceasing. In what ways do you live as if this were not true?

Lesson

6

EXERCISE

WHAT IS IT
IN YOUR JAR?

15 minutes

The Israelites kept some manna in a jar as a way to remember how God provided for them. God has given us reminders, too. Spend a few minutes silently answering these questions about the "manna" in your jar.

1. What things come to mind that you would like to bottle for the rest of your life so you never are a day without them? (It can be anything—something tangible, or a feeling or desire.)
2. If God was filling the jar as a lifelong gift for you, what things do you think he would put in the jar to help you remember his goodness?
3. What life events would go into your jar as reminders of God's faithfulness to you?
4. What Scripture or promises from God's Word should go into the jar to help you always remember who Jesus is for you?

Now discuss with the group how the jar you filled up compares to how you imagine God would fill a jar for you. What does this tell you about yourself?

WRAP-UP AND PRAYER *5 minutes*

Use the promises and verses from question 4 in the exercise to guide your prayer time. Thank God for his promises and ask him to help you trust them.

7

WATER FROM THE ROCK

BIG IDEA

We can be sure of Jesus in all situations because he is our true Rock, who took the judgment we deserve and gives us life.

BIBLE CONVERSATION *20 minutes*

How would it feel to be wrongly accused or judged unfairly? Or what if someone else was blamed for something you had done. How would you feel?

In today's passage we will read of one who was falsely accused and could have felt the same way you have but acted quite differently than you would expect. Have someone read **Exodus 17:1–7** out loud.

The word for *quarreling* in the original Hebrew language carries the connotation of a courtroom scene. With this view in mind, how do you think the Israelites' accusations against Moses would hold up in court today?

What do you think Moses was feeling toward the Israelites and God, and why?

Although the passage says the people tested the Lord, what can we say is true about God by the fact that he still provided water for them?

* * * *

Today's article will help you understand what was happening when Moses struck the rock. Read it out loud together, taking turns at the paragraph breaks.

Lesson

ARTICLE

THE THIRSTY ONE

5 minutes

Even if you've never sat in a courtroom during a trial, you've likely seen one play out on television or in a movie. When it's time for a verdict, the defendant rises and stands before the judge, who may strike with his gavel as a symbol of judgment when he announces his decision. The rest of the courtroom is mostly filled with those who want to see the defendant pay.

The scene in Exodus 17 is similar: the people turned against Moses and were ready to find him guilty and punish him, though Moses pointed out their real quarrel was against God. The people claimed God was not with them or meeting their needs, not keeping his covenant.

A covenant is an irrevocable promise, similar to our legal contracts but even more binding. Early in the Bible, God made a covenant with Adam and Eve, promising life but warning of death if they disobeyed him. When they broke that covenant, God showed grace and made a new promise of the one who would redeem us and make all things right again. Then with Noah, God made a covenant promising never to send another deadly worldwide flood. And with Abram (later called Abraham), God made a covenant promising many descendants and a land for them to call home.

In creating that covenant, God told Abram to kill animals and cut them into pieces, arranging the bloody parts to make a path through the middle. The custom was for each party to the covenant to walk between the animal parts as a binding promise to keep their end of the deal or be killed like the cut-up animals. It was serious! But then God passed through the animal pieces *alone*. In doing so, he alone took *all* responsibility to keep the promises.

Now let's shift back to the wilderness with the Israelites. God's covenant promise to Abram included them, Abram's descendants. But God had not yet delivered them to the land as promised, and now they seemed about to die of thirst. Could this be what was fueling their anger? It seems what they saw as God's failure to make good on his promise had become their evidence for the courtroom scene we are witnessing.

Remember, the consequence for a broken covenant is death, which means the Israelites were asking that Moses receive a death sentence. Ironically, it was them—the ones pressing charges—who deserved death. The defendant was innocent. But the Israelites' shortsighted self-centeredness was lost on them. All they could see was the failure of Moses, God's representative, to make good on his promised deliverance.

Isn't that just like us? Not getting what we want, when we want it, or how we want it, we accuse God of neglect. We think he has forgotten us. So instead of trusting his Word to be true, we turn to false gods. We try to control our circumstances and save ourselves from the hopelessness or emptiness we often feel.

Amazingly, God does not throw our guilt back in our faces. Instead he faithfully gives us himself. You see, in every way we neglect him and fall short of God's perfect standard, he was perfect *for* us. He declared at the cross, "It is finished." This was his guarantee to believers that we are sealed in God's permanent love and acceptance.

To gently remind the Israelites *again* of his faithfulness, God reintroduced an object they would remember vividly. If you recall, all the water in Egypt turned to blood after Moses struck the Nile River with his staff.

That was a sign of God's judgment against Egypt. Now the staff again came out for judgment. This time, to put an end to the mob mentality of the Israelites, God told Moses to strike the rock with the staff.

But who was on that rock? Who stood before the judge? God had told Moses, "I will stand before you there on the rock at Horeb, and you shall strike the rock" (Exodus 17:6). It's as if God said, "Bring the judgment on me! I will receive the blow of justice that my people deserve." And when God did that, water gushed out of the rock to save his people from death.

What a picture of Jesus! Look at the wonders to which this incident points.

- Jesus is our rock in the wilderness. In all of our struggles on this earth, he is the firm place to go. "The LORD is my rock and my fortress and my deliverer, my God, my rock, in whom I take refuge" (Psalm 18:2).
- Jesus is our substitute defendant. He stood before the judge and was condemned in our place, taking the punishment we deserve.
- Jesus is our source of spiritual water. He is the Savior who gives us life out of death. When he died on the cross, a soldier pierced his side, just as Moses struck the rock, and water flowed out of him.

On that cross, right before he declared all was finished, Jesus cried out, "I thirst." He went thirsty so we could drink deeply from the waters of his grace that flow from the ultimate hard place—not a rock, but the cross. He saves us from death like he did for the Israelites, who "all drank the same spiritual drink. For they drank from the spiritual Rock that followed them, and the Rock was Christ" (1 Corinthians 10:3–4).

DISCUSSION *10 minutes*

When have you seen yourself carrying on like the Israelites, demanding that God act according to how you see fit? What do you think is at the root of your anger with God?

What are your deepest fears when it feels like God has left you in the wilderness and you can't see him at work?

Ultimately, assurance is given to us at the cross. As Moses struck the rock in judgment, Jesus—our Rock—took that same judgment on himself in our place. Because he did, instead of receiving God's wrath as the penalty for our sin, we receive grace upon grace upon grace poured out on us by Jesus. Where do you see the water of his grace in your life?

Lesson

EXERCISE

ROCK OF AGES

15 minutes

In many verses in the Psalms and elsewhere in Scripture, we are told more about how God is our rock. In this exercise, you will first spend a few minutes looking through some Bible verses on your own. Later you will share your observations with the group.

Begin by thinking about your doubts. Note a time you have had feelings like those expressed in the two verses below.

> **Psalm 28:1**
>
> To you, O Lord, I call;
> > my rock, be not deaf to me,
> lest, if you be silent to me,
> > I become like those who go down to the pit.

every day when all I want to do is die

> **Psalm 42:9**
>
> I say to God, my rock:
> > "Why have you forgotten me?
> Why do I go mourning
> > because of the oppression of the enemy?"

when everyone else seems to have a plan

Now read through the verses below on your own. As you read, circle or highlight words in each verse that tell you who Jesus is as your rock, or make notes about what it means that Jesus is your rock.

but i don't

60

Deuteronomy 32:4

> The Rock, his work is perfect,
>> for all his ways are justice.
> A God of faithfulness and without iniquity,
>> just and upright is he.

1 Samuel 2:2

> There is none holy like the LORD,
>> there is none besides you;
>> there is no rock like our God.

2 Samuel 22:47

> The LORD lives, and blessed be my rock,
>> and exalted be my God, the rock of my salvation.

Psalm 18:2

> The LORD is my rock and my fortress and my deliverer,
>> my God, my rock, in whom I take refuge,
>> my shield, and the horn of my salvation, my stronghold.

Psalm 31:1–3

> In you, O LORD, do I take refuge;
>> let me never be put to shame;
>> in your righteousness deliver me!
> Incline your ear to me;
>> rescue me speedily!
> Be a rock of refuge for me,
>> a strong fortress to save me!
> For you are my rock and my fortress;
>> and for your name's sake you lead me and guide me.

Psalm 62:7

> On God rests my salvation and my glory;
>> my mighty rock, my refuge is God.

Psalm 71:3

> Be to me a rock of refuge,
>> to which I may continually come;
> you have given the command to save me,
>> for you are my rock and my fortress.

Psalm 78:35

> They remembered that God was their rock,
>> the Most High God their Redeemer.

Psalm 92:15

> Declare that the LORD is upright;
>> he is my rock, and there is no unrighteousness in him.

Psalm 144:1

> Blessed be the LORD, my rock,
>> who trains my hands for war,
>> and my fingers for battle.

1 Peter 2:4–6

As you come to him, a living stone rejected by men but in the sight of God chosen and precious, you yourselves like living stones are being built up as a spiritual house, to be a holy priesthood, to offer spiritual sacrifices acceptable to God through Jesus Christ. For it stands in Scripture:

> "Behold, I am laying in Zion a stone,
>> a cornerstone chosen and precious,
> and whoever believes in him will not be put to shame."

In the midst of trials, suffering, sin, and temptations, it is easy for our self-talk to become an inner dialogue of anger and despair. What we need then is to be reoriented back to the truth of who God is and his promises to us. Hopefully, next time your inner lawyer starts to draw up charges against him, you will recall from this exercise what it means that Christ is your rock.

Now share with the group some of the words you underlined or noted about what it means for Jesus to be your rock.

Which of these words is most meaningful to you, or gives you a new appreciation for Jesus? Why? Share what it means to you.

WRAP-UP AND PRAYER *5 minutes*

Before you leave, choose a few of the verses above to memorize. Start working on them now, and commit to learn them so that you have this truth tucked away the next time you need assurance Jesus is with you and for you. Later, you might also want to dwell on some of these specific words. For example, you could write in a prayer journal how Jesus is your *refuge*, or do a word study to find other places Scripture uses that word.

Then finish by spending a few minutes in prayer, asking God to help you trust him as your rock, fortress, and deliverer.

8

COVENANT CONFIRMED

BIG IDEA

God binds himself to his people and establishes them as his treasured possession through the giving of the Law.

BIBLE CONVERSATION *20 minutes*

What are some of the rules in your house? Do you find them a joy to follow? Why or why not?

Many people view the Bible as a book of rules and see God to be like Pharaoh—an angry taskmaster telling us what to do. But just as your parents put rules in place because they love you and want to protect you, God gives commands to his people not to spoil their fun but to make their lives good.

Read **Exodus 19:1–20**, where God prepares his people to receive the Ten Commandments. (Have a few people in your group read the passage aloud.)

Do you believe God considers you as his treasured possession? Why or why not?

All the instructions given to the people about preparation tell us we have to be careful about the way we approach God. Why do you think we must be so careful with God?

What do you think it was like for the Israelites to witness this scene of God's presence descending on the mountain?

Our second reading picks up after God gave the Ten Commandments and all his laws to Moses, and he came down the mountain to share these with the people. Turn to **Exodus 24:3–8,** and have someone read it out loud.

Do you think it's possible for the people to obey all that God commanded as they said they would? Why or why not?

****

Once again, we have a pointer to something greater coming. Read the article aloud together, taking turns at the paragraph breaks.

SAVED AND KEPT BY GOD

5 minutes

Throughout Exodus, we have seen God's faithfulness to the Israelites—in Egypt, through the Red Sea, and even amid their grumbling in the wilderness. Now, to confirm his love and formalize their status as his chosen people, he is giving them his Law.

It may seem strange that giving his Law is how he intends to seal his love for them since we think of laws as restricting. But God's purposes are like your parents putting rules in place because they love you. God's Law will solidify and confirm his covenant relationship with his people. And it will give them a way to live that is, as Psalm 19:10 says, more desired than gold and sweeter than honey.

As we've learned, God is the sole initiator of his covenants and the one who makes sure they are kept. When he covenanted with Abraham, he alone walked between the sacrificed animals to symbolically display taking full responsibility for upholding both ends of the covenant. This is imperative to rightly understanding God's declaration to the Israelites that they will be his treasured possession, kingdom priest, and holy nation *if they obey and keep his commands.*

This statement sounds conditional on their obedience. Isn't this how we too often think about our standing before God? If we do what he requires, we expect he should be pleased with us and make things go our way. We live as if we earn his blessings or curses by how we behave. So, we try to use being good as a way to manipulate God and control our lives—as if we were God. We live as if God operates under the mantra *you get what you deserve.*

This is why we need gospel glasses to understand that *if you obey and keep my commands* is not a conditional clause. God's love is not based on us being worthy. Remember, by the time of the exodus God has already made his covenant. The Israelites *are* his chosen people. He did not set his love on them because of anything they did, nor did he remove his love because of anything they failed to do. Their obedience was not what kept their status as God's people; their obedience was a sign they already had status as God's people.

God is saying their obedience to the Law is a reflection of their love. This is one reason he gives his Law—so we know how we *can* reflect back our special status as God's most prized possessions. His Law is like a letter telling us what delights him. You could call it God's love language.

Think of it as your mom telling you what she wants you to do for her on Mother's Day. You want to do what she desires because of how much she does for you all year to show you love. The fact she told you what she wants is awesome because now you know just how you can please her. To reflect her love back to her shows her your love.

Of course, despite being God's treasured possessions, we don't always obey God's laws and treasure him above all things. This is because of the sin that still lives within us. But thankfully, he doesn't remove his love from us even though the penalty for disobedience is still death.

God does not judge us because, in his goodness to faithfully uphold his covenant, he sent his Son to suffer that penalty instead. Jesus became the sacrifice, the one torn in two, for our failure to keep God's laws. So now, even in our sin, we stand secure in a right relationship with God. God accepts us as his children according to Jesus's righteousness.

We are covered and cleaned by his blood shed for us. This is the very picture we are given when Moses sprinkled the people saying, "Behold the blood of the covenant that the LORD has made with you" (Exodus 24:8). They had promised to do all God commanded and meant it with all their hearts, but perfect obedience was not something they could ever attain. It was Jesus, centuries later, who finally kept that promise. He became the only Israelite to perfectly obey God. And at the Last Supper he lifted his cup and said, "This is my blood of the covenant" (Mark 14:24).

Today when communion is served, Jesus's same words are used in remembrance of his blood shed for our covenant unfaithfulness. Despite our sin, we don't have to fear God's rejection. Jesus did everything God requires, and we belong to Jesus! It is not our good works that make us right with God, but Jesus's perfect work. We get his righteousness; he took our sin.

This great exchange is what separates Christianity from every other religion. In no other religion could someone else merit righteousness in the place of another, but the true God operates on a completely different economy or system, and it's called grace. Grace is the premise of God's covenant that sets us apart as his holy nation—a nation delighted to serve our King!

It doesn't make sense that we get what we so clearly don't deserve. But when we begin to grasp the truth of all God has done for covenant breakers like us, that truth leads us to want to obey his Law as an expression of our gratitude.

DISCUSSION *10 minutes*

In what ways do you see yourself trying to gain God's favor through your obedience?

When you have disobeyed, or become aware of your sin, how have you felt like God views you? What makes it hard to believe God's love never wavers even in your sin?

Why is grace hard for us to accept?

Lesson

EXERCISE

IS HE SAFE?

15 minutes

In C. S. Lewis's famous book, *The Lion, The Witch and The Wardrobe*, Mr. Beaver tells the children Aslan is on the move. They sense this must mean either a terrible nightmare or the best dream ever, and they ask more about Aslan. They learn he is Lord of the Woods and a lion, which causes one child to ask whether he is safe.

To this, Mrs. Beaver replies, "If there is anyone who can appear before Aslan without their knees knocking, they're either braver than most or else just silly."

Mr. Beaver adds, "Safe? . . . Who said anything about safe? 'Course he isn't safe. But he's good. He's the King, I tell you."[1]

C. S. Lewis intended Aslan to be a fantasy-world representation of Jesus, the same Lord of heaven and earth who came down at Mount Sinai. Considering this, discuss the following questions.

1. What do you think makes Aslan unsafe?
2. If he is unsafe, how can he also be good? What do you think C. S. Lewis meant by *he isn't safe but he's good*?
3. How do you see this scene from *The Lion, The Witch and The Wardrobe* relating to our passage in Exodus?

---

1. C. S. Lewis, *The Lion, The Witch and The Wardrobe* (New York: Collier, 1970), 75–76.

4. How do you think the Israelites viewed God when they were standing at the base of the mountain amid the thunder, lightning, and blasting trumpets? Why?
5. What do you think a proper fear of God looks like for God's children?

WRAP-UP AND PRAYER *5 minutes*

We've seen God to be a God of both judgment and wrath, and a God of great grace and mercy. On the one hand, he is so holy the Israelites could not even touch the mountain. At the same time, he came down to draw near and solidify a relationship with the people he calls his children—because he is good.

Children feel welcomed and affectionately loved by earthly fathers. Because they have received a father's love so readily, this also leads them to be respectful of his standards and please him in all they do. So, too, is our posture before God. By the sound of his voice he created all things and in the palm of his hand holds all power. To think this same God invites us to draw near should cause us to tremble, but to tremble in awe and with great praise that he withdrew judgment from us and adopted us as heirs of his kingdom!

Because of this truth, you can leave this lesson full of thanksgiving and a greater desire to live for God's glory, not so much because you owe it back to him, but out of gratitude for all he has done for you.

As part of your prayer time today, spend a few minutes praising God for making you his treasured possession. Ask him to help you treasure him above all things. If there's a specific part of obeying his Law you're struggling with, ask him for help. He isn't with you to condemn you, but to help you.

Lesson

9

THE LAW DECONSTRUCTED

BIG IDEA

God's Law shows us the true condition of our hearts and how much we need Jesus's perfect record for us.

BIBLE CONVERSATION *20 minutes*

On a scale from one to ten, with ten being the best, where would you rank in how well you keep God's commandments? Explain why you ranked yourself where you did.

If you discover during today's lesson you were off the mark in your self-evaluation, that's okay. The purpose is not to make you feel bad but to help you see how much we need Jesus as the perfect commandment keeper for us. Remember from last week, our obedience is how we can show our love back to God, not the basis of our standing.

Now read **Exodus 20:1–17** out loud, taking turns a few verses at a time.

The Ten Commandments can be summed up under two headings. These are stated in Matthew 22:37–39, "You shall love the Lord your God with all your heart and with all your soul and with all your mind.

This is the great and first commandment. And a second is like it: You shall love your neighbor as yourself."

Based on that summary, which commandments would you put under the heading *Love Your God* and which ones under the heading *Love Your Neighbor*?

If you fail to love your neighbor in any way, why would it also be true that you have broken the first commandment, "You shall have no other gods before me"? What do you think this commandment wants us to see about ourselves?

∗ ∗ ∗ ∗

To learn more about the perfect standard God's commands require, read the article "The Law as a Mirror." (Read it aloud, taking turns at the paragraph breaks.)

THE LAW
AS A MIRROR

5 minutes

Peyton is a "good" kid. She doesn't party or hang out with kids who do. She is respectful in class, turns her work in on time, and makes good grades. Her family regularly attends church, and she is also involved in the youth group. Never does she appear to have a bad day, or at least no one would ever know if she did because she is always smiling and encouraging others.

Joey attends the same church as Peyton, but he doesn't like to go to youth group. He feels judged by many of the kids, including Peyton, who seem so perfect. He assumes rightly that they think he's not a good Christian because of who his friends are and his drinking at parties. Though he knows others' acceptance is one of his biggest idols, he still keeps trying to fit in and look cool. He constantly repents, and yet he does what he doesn't want to do.

Looking at Peyton's performance, we might conclude that she is the more spiritual one. But even from this little snapshot we can see that *both* she and Joey have broken the first commandment to have no God but the Lord. Peyton likely doesn't realize it. Because she follows outward rules, she doesn't see that she has made an idol out of herself—basing her worth on her own self-effort. Because of this, she is blind to inward sins, such as pride, and feels little need for Jesus's worth and work for her.

Joey, on the other hand, sees his idol. Because he knows other people's opinions rule him as a functional god, he is actually in a better place than Peyton. He sees his sin and knows he needs Jesus. He may continue to struggle, but the fact that he feels convicted by his sin is evidence of God's grace working in his life.

In the last lesson, we learned that one reason God gives us commands is to show us how to live as his children. Another reason God gives commands is for them to serve as a mirror, reflecting back to us what is in our hearts. When we see what God requires of us and face the reality of how we fall short, this should drive us to Jesus who lived a sinless life *for* us.

We can't obey perfectly; only Jesus did. But if we view the Ten Commandments as simply a list of outward dos and don'ts, we might fall into Peyton's trap of thinking we are good by our own effort. To realize how desperately we need Jesus, we must see how the Ten Commandments cut below the surface and drive at the motives of our hearts. We've touched on this with the idolatry behind the first commandment to have no other gods. Now let's take a closer look at the others.

You shall not make and worship images. This commandment is about worshiping God incorrectly. We do this when we fashion him into someone we wish him to be. For example, we may only want to see him as a God of love and not a God who hates sin, so we reimagine him to be a sweet grandpa or the Santa Claus who gives according to our goodness, and we ignore that he is a holy God.

You shall not take the Lord's name in vain. This commandment means more than not using God's name as a swear word, though that is included. It's also about hypocrisy. When we claim to be Christians but defame God's name with ungodly behavior or fake devotion, we're taking his name in vain.

Remember the Sabbath day. *Sabbath* means "rest." God created the world in six days, but the seventh day he called holy, a day of rest. The Sabbath is given to us as a gift to break from our daily concerns and work and re-center our self-focused lives back on him. But in our busy schedules, we easily neglect the Sabbath's intended purpose and God's command.

Honor your father and mother. Even when we honor our parents or God with our words and actions, our hearts can still be full of rebellion or resentment. This puts Jesus's perfect obedience as a boy in perspective. He never disrespected his mom or dad *for you* because he knew you would fail in this area.

You shall not murder. This covers the way we treat every human being. If we dismiss someone, wish harm on someone, or act coldly toward someone, we have failed to love our neighbor. We kill people in our hearts through anger, pride, indifference, and neglect. Could it be, then, that Peyton's judgment of Joey (which kept him away from youth group) broke this commandment?

You shall not commit adultery. This commandment includes more than physical adultery; it requires purity in thoughts, words, and actions. It means keeping the body pure, as a temple to God and for a future spouse. It involves how we dress, seek attention, and conduct ourselves in relationships, making it relevant whether or not we are yet married.

You shall not steal. This commandment requires we not acquire money and material things unlawfully, unethically, or greedily. This makes cheating on a test stealing by taking answers that aren't yours. In the workplace, this could be spending time online shopping instead of working, which steals an employer's time.

You shall not bear false witness. Our desire to look better than others makes us all guilty according to this commandment. We must not lie, slander, or spread gossip, and we should take a stand against gossip and mocking on behalf of others.

You shall not covet. Coveting means wanting something that isn't ours, so this rule means our desires must be godly along with our actions. Breaking this commandment—or any of the others—means we also break the first commandment because we've made a heart-level idol our functional god.

It's hard to look in the mirror and see how dirty we are with sin. But seeing ourselves rightly is the only way we will know how much we need to grab the soap—that is Jesus, who makes us clean. Amazingly, when we grab onto Jesus we get his spotless record instead of our filthy one! That's right: Jesus kept every one of these commands perfectly—and his record is yours. So even if the Ten Commandments show you're a bigger sinner than you thought, they shouldn't make you feel more condemned. If they cause you to give up trusting yourself and instead trust Jesus, they will actually help you know that you are forgiven, blameless, and delightfully clean in Christ.

DISCUSSION *10 minutes*

After reading the article, would you still rate yourself the same as you did at the beginning of the lesson, or would you score yourself differently on the one to ten scale? If your score would be different now, what did you hear that changed your view?

Did you identify more with Peyton, Joey, or neither one, and why?

Why do you think it is important to see the intent behind the Ten Commandments and why they go deeper than just external behavior?

TAKING THE LAW TO HEART

15 minutes

Each of the Ten Commandments from our passage is listed below. Spend some time on your own coming up with a specific example of how a typical teen (this includes you!) might be tempted to violate each commandment, either in actions or heart attitudes. When you finish, discuss your examples as a group.

1. You shall have no other gods before me. *putting high School life above God*

2. You shall not make for yourself a carved image. *depending on your friends to be fine to go to Church*

3. You shall not take the name of the Lord your God in vain. *Saying you go to church but then being the mean girl at school*

4. Remember the Sabbath day, to keep it holy. Spending time w/ friends bc its a wknd instead of focusing on God

5. Honor your father and mother. doing somthing they would say no to but just not asking them

6. You shall not murder. hating your sibling, or that 1 weird kid in class

7. You shall not commit adultery. the amount of weight that is put on your virginity/ sexuality

8. You shall not steal. Cheating, shoplifting

9. You shall not bear false witness against your neighbor. Spreading rumors, lying to make yourself look better

10. You shall not covet. _Wanting for friends_
Gucci belt

Remember, we break the first commandment every time we break any other commandment, because breaking any of the others means there is an idol in our hearts we have decided to serve instead of serving God.

Consider commandments three through ten once more. Discuss what might be the heart desire (an idol!) that causes a person to take God's name in vain.

> To ignore Sabbath rest?
> To dishonor their father and mother?
> To murder, harm, or hate someone?
> To be sexually impure?
> To steal, cheat, or be greedy?
> To lie or gossip?
> To covet?

WRAP-UP AND PRAYER 5 minutes

It's important that instead of feeling beaten up by your study of the commandments, you gain greater appreciation for all Jesus does for you. As you pray, ask God to use his commands to show you what's true about your heart. Ask that instead of relying on your own power to try harder, you will rely on Jesus and believe better.

There is some outside reading to do before the next lesson because it will be too much to read during the meeting. **Before the next session, read chapters 25 through 31 in Exodus.**

Lesson

10

TABERNACLE

BIG IDEA

The tabernacle shows how Jesus is central to all of life.

BIBLE CONVERSATION *20 minutes*

This past week you were asked to read Exodus 25—31 about the building of the tent of worship called the tabernacle. The fact that there is so much detail about the tabernacle over the course of these chapters should signal that the detail is something God wants us to pay attention to.

Considering the amount of detail God gave, what do you think he wants us to know about himself and our worship of him?

Let's review some of the events you have already studied in Exodus.

- God descended onto Mount Sinai amid thunder, lightning, and trumpets.
- Moses went up into God's presence to receive the Law.
- God confirmed his covenant with the sprinkling of blood. Then Moses went back up the mountain where he remained for forty days, receiving instructions for the tabernacle.

This is where your study lands today. The context is important because, as you will see, we must not separate God's earlier commands about how to live from his instructions now about the tabernacle. But remember that the Israelites were not yet to the Promised Land, so this tabernacle was not a permanent structure. It was a tent to go with them on their journey because God wanted to dwell with them in their midst.

Begin by reading **Exodus 25:1–9**. (Have someone read this aloud.)

How do these specific materials make you think about being in God's presence?

To better understand God's building requirements, have someone in the group read each of the following passages aloud.

Exodus 25:10–11, 31

Exodus 26:1–12

Exodus 27:1–3, 9–10, 20

As you heard, absolutely no detail is left to the imagination of the people. God prescribes it exactly as he wants it done. There is a reason for this, which our article will unpack. But first read these two passages that tell what happened after the Israelites followed all of God's instructions.

Exodus 40:1–9

Exodus 40:16–38

What do you think it must have been like for the Israelites to see God's glory actually come down and dwell in their midst?

＊＊＊＊

You've just read how Exodus ends, with God coming to dwell with his people in the tabernacle. But there's still more to understand about the tabernacle, so read the article aloud, taking turns at the paragraph breaks.

Lesson

ARTICLE

TABERNACLE UNVEILED

5 minutes

Have you ever watched a parent try to put something together without instructions and get toward the end before they realize they messed up? Maybe it was a recipe that should have been followed exactly but wasn't. Or what if a builder strayed from the house plans? One missed step, ingredient, or alteration would throw the whole thing off.

God, too, had specific instructions for the tabernacle, for a specific reason. God's people may not simply worship him however they please. In the case of the Israelites, God gave details about required sacrifices and holy days. And here in Exodus, his details include colors, dimensions, materials, arrangements, tools used, and even where hemlines must fall. The tabernacle was to be a place for God to dwell with his people—where heaven meets earth! It was important to portray such a wonder the way God instructed.

What, then, does the tabernacle tell us about worship? Let's look at it starting with the innermost room and working out from there.

The Most Holy Place was the shape of a perfect cube, a pointer to the perfection of God. It was completely enclosed by blue curtains to represent heaven, and separated from the rest of the inner tent by a thick curtain called the veil. The only furnishing in the room was the ark, made of wood and pure gold. Inside the ark were the Ten Commandments. The ark's lid was an atonement cover that symbolized how, through sacrifices, God covered his people's failure to keep his commands. No one was allowed in the Most Holy Place except the high priest, once a year on the Day of Atonement, and only following God's prescribed rules so that the priest wouldn't be struck dead. When he did enter, the high priest sprinkled blood from a sacrifice on the cover of the ark.

The Holy Place was the next room out. It contained three objects: a lampstand to the left of the entrance, a table of showbread on the right, and an altar of incense. Each was made of wood and pure gold. Only the priests were permitted in this room. They kept the bread fresh and made sure the light never stopped burning, day or night. They also burned incense at the altar near the entrance to the Most Holy Place, offering up prayers on behalf of the people.

The courtyard outside surrounded those tabernacle rooms. There was a bronze altar at the entrance to the courtyard and a bronze washing basin just beyond it, so that the materials used were less valuable further out from the center. Priests came daily to offer sacrifices on the altar, and would wash themselves at the basin before entering the Holy Place. The people congregated in the courtyard and brought their own sacrifices there. Once inside the courtyard, no one could miss hearing or smelling the sacrifices. This too was by God's design, to engage the people's senses with an awareness of his presence and centrality.

The camp, where the people lived, surrounded all of it. This meant everything centered on God. His presence was constantly before them, as it should be with us. Worship is integral to who we are as God's people. This means our church attendance and the way we worship God is important, but it is more than church—it is life as worship. We center our lives around him being with us.

But the revelation God gave about the tabernacle, the mediation of the priests, and the sacrificial system is an incomplete picture. It's only a pointer to what we now know through life in Christ. In Hebrews 8, the tabernacle, the priests, the Law, and the sacrifices are called copies and shadows. The Israelites were able to enjoy fellowship with God through his dwelling in the tabernacle among them—but not fully. God's full dwelling with his people was coming later, through Jesus.

John 1:14 says about Jesus, "the Word became flesh and dwelt among us." The Greek derivative of that word *dwell* is related to the Hebrew word for "pitching a tent." And the Greek verb *to tent* resembles the Hebrew word *shekinah*, used to describe God's glory. So what John tells us upon Jesus's arrival is, "The Word became flesh and *tabernacled* among us." In other words, Jesus is the shekinah glory that filled the tabernacle in Exodus 40. He is the true tabernacle.

In Jesus, heaven and earth meet. Jesus fulfills everything in the tabernacle from the ark to the altar, as the exercise you'll do later will point out.

After the people completed every detail of the work on the tabernacle, God's glory descended on the ark. That's how the book of Exodus ends—with a big finish. But the people still had to stay back from God, separated by the veil, meaning a bigger finish with one changed detail was yet to come.

After Jesus finished everything necessary to secure our right standing before God, he offered himself as the final sacrifice so we would have full access into God's presence. As Jesus died for us, the veil in the temple was torn in two from top to bottom. God himself tore it because no longer would anything separate us from him. Now there is open access into God's presence through faith in Jesus, whose work was sufficient.

DISCUSSION *10 minutes*

What do you think it means that life is worship? How do we fail to live as if life is worship?

Many people today think of worship as only the singing portion of a church service, but Scripture teaches that our bodies are temples of the Holy Spirit and our lives are to be a reflection of this indwelling spirit within us. Therefore, everything we do should be centered on God's presence in our lives. That is why it is said we have a holy and high calling in all that we do. Even being a hardworking student striving to do your best brings glory to God and is, in this sense, worship.

What are some other everyday "non-spiritual" things you could call acts of worship?

Why do you think God gave his people the tabernacle at the same time he gave the Ten Commandments?

If you recall, the Law is like a mirror imaging forth what is in our hearts so that we see our sin accurately, along with our deep need for a Savior. After hearing the Law, the Israelites may have felt beaten up. They didn't know—but we do now—that we have a Savior who perfectly met the Law's requirements so we are free from the Law. This is why our obedience is not the condition for God's love. Considering the Israelites didn't know Christ's perfection for them, to hear God wanted to dwell among them would have been welcome confirmation that he was for them and planned to be with them. This is good news and calls for greater worship.

Lesson

EXERCISE

THE TRUE TABERNACLE

15 minutes

Look at the diagram of the tabernacle and the list of its parts and furnishings. See if you can match the items in the list with parts of the diagram. Refer back to today's article if necessary.

LIST

Gold altar of incense

Bronze altar of sacrifice

Ark with atonement cover

Lampstand

Courtyard gate

Courtyard

Priest

Table of showbread

Holy Place

Most Holy Place

Veil

Washing basin

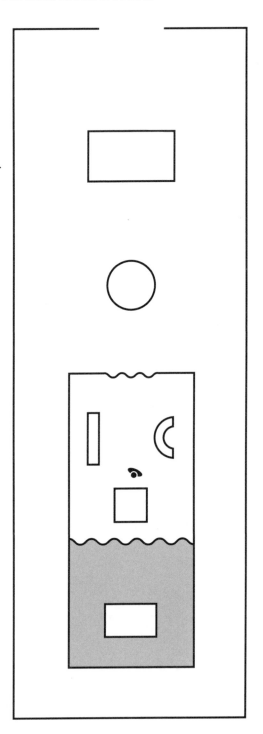

Now use words from the list to fill in the blanks below that show how Jesus perfectly fulfilled parts of tabernacle worship. (Not every word will be used.)

The _Courtyard gate_

points to how Jesus is the only way into God's presence.

The _washing basin_

shows how Jesus washes and cleanses us as the Living Water.

The _priest_

points to Jesus our only mediator, who prays for us.

The _lampstand_

shows how Jesus is the Light of the World.

The _table of showbread_

shows how Jesus is the Bread of Life.

The _Bronze alter of sacrifice_

points to the place where Jesus's blood was poured out for our sin.

The _Gold altar of incense_

points to Jesus's life and death, a pleasing aroma that rises to God's throne and intercedes with the Father on our behalf.

Now discuss your answers. What were the most powerful connections to Jesus for you to see?

WRAP-UP AND PRAYER *5 minutes*

Summarize what you heard and your main takeaways from this lesson. As you pray, ask God to help you keep him central in your life, and to help you make all you do worship of him.

Lesson

11

A GOLDEN IDOL

BIG IDEA

We all turn to false gods, but God in his gracious mercy sent his Son as the propitiation for our sin, to make us his people.

BIBLE CONVERSATION *20 minutes*

Can you think of a time you did something wrong you never thought you would do? If you are willing, tell about that.

Before God confirmed his covenant with the people, Moses had come down off the mountain to read God's Law to them. Upon hearing it, you may remember they responded with, "All the words that the Lord has spoken we will do."

Well, today you will see just how long that lasted after Moses went back up on the mountain. You will also see how prone we are to turn away from the God we say we love. (Have some in your group read the following passages aloud.)

Exodus 32:1–16

Exodus 32:19–24

Exodus 32:30–35

Why do you think the people so quickly neglected their promise to keep all of God's commands? What does this say about what ruled their hearts?

After hearing what the people had done, what did you think about Moses's plea for God to show them mercy? Do you think he was defending their sin? How would you have responded?

Moses was a mediator. He acted to make peace between the people and God. This will be further discussed in the article, but with this in mind, why do you think God referred to the Israelites as Moses's people instead of saying *my people* or *my children*?

* * * *

Now take turns reading the article out loud.

11

ARTICLE

THE MEDIATOR

5 minutes

Have you ever been upset over the sin of a close friend, but were quick to defend your friend if someone talked negatively about her? Perhaps it's because you know your love for your friend won't change, but you don't want others to see your friend's sin because you don't know how they'll respond. You don't want anyone to judge, dismiss, or gossip about your friend. So you jump in loyally, to protect.

This is how it was with Moses and the Israelites. Remember, initially Moses insisted he was not the right man for Israel. But through trials and suffering and years spent together, he had grown to love and care for the people. So now, even after they built a golden calf, Moses was still for them. He didn't defend their actions, but he did plead with God to be gracious despite what they had done.

Not because Moses wasn't angry—he obviously was. As soon as he got down the mountain and saw the golden calf, his fury caused him to throw down and break the tablets God had given him to take back to the people. Don't miss the irony in this: these were the tablets of God's commandments, the very laws the people had promised to uphold.

Instead of keeping their word not to worship a graven image, take God's name in vain, or put any other gods before him, they created their own god. It was a calf, of all things—weak and lowly—perhaps because they wanted to make a god that seemed easy to control. But set before them now was the tablet with a big crack running through it as a visual reminder of their brokenness and inability to keep God's commands.

The people should have known God cannot be controlled. But when Moses took too long to come down off the mountain, they grew restless, faithless, and impatient. Aaron, as one of the men left in charge, should have pointed them back to remembering who God is, but instead he made it easy for the people to sin. Of course, when Moses questioned him, he attempted to excuse himself from responsibility: The calf just popped out. It was the people's fault. "You know the people, that they are set on evil" (Exodus 32:22).

The truth is, without the intervening work of the Spirit we are all set on sin. It is our human heart condition. So, when God referred to the Israelites as a stiff-necked people, the same could be said of us. What this means is even worse than you think. The dictionary defines *stiff-necked* as lordly, masterful, self-asserting, authoritarian, dominant, narcissistic, prideful, and self-centered.[1] In other words, the Israelites wanted to take things into their own hands, be their own god, and do whatever suited their own desires. While for us it isn't a golden calf, we too resurrect our own false gods and try to take control, thinking our ways better than God's even though he is always faithful.

The gold the Israelites used to form the calf was the very gold God *provided* when he instructed them to plunder the Egyptians before escaping out of slavery. How quickly they forgot the one who had redeemed them and bound himself to be their God.

But God knew this about the people. We've seen it throughout Exodus. And while God has always met his people's sin with unwavering love, this time we are left wondering for a moment if they went too far. But when God sent Moses down to deal with the people and the consequences, it was never that he was ready to break covenant; that would be

---

1. *Merriam-Webster's Collegiate Dictionary*, 11th ed., s.v. "stiff-necked."

against his very nature. However, his anger showed us the seriousness of sin. It could not go unpunished.

Fast-forward to a time much later in history when Jesus, only hours before his arrest and crucifixion, lifted his eyes up to heaven and begged God to set apart his children and make them holy. He said, "For their sake I consecrate myself, that they also may be sanctified in truth" (John 17:19). To consecrate something means to set it aside for a holy purpose. Jesus was giving himself up to God's plan to take the punishment we deserved.

Remember that Moses consecrated the people, too. Before God came to them at Mount Sinai, they washed their garments as an outward sign of being prepared to receive his Law. But what about their inward sin? What about their stiff-necked hearts and the idolatry it would bring?

What was then only an outward sign of holiness becomes an inward reality through Jesus. After Jesus met every requirement of God's commands, he laid down his life for his people. His holy, perfect life is now credited to all God's people for all time, even though we don't deserve it. When Moses pleaded for the Israelites, who did not deserve grace, he was a pointer to the true mediator—Jesus, who makes peace between us and God.

The Israelites would still suffer consequences of their sin, as we do. But isn't it amazing that God didn't hold their sin against them? Instead, he continued his faithfulness to bless a faithless, fickle people who profaned his name. This means we, too, can rest in Jesus. Despite our sinful and idolatrous hearts, God's anger has been appeased, and we are covered permanently in Christ's righteousness.

DISCUSSION *10 minutes*

How was Aaron's answer when he was caught in sin like Eve's answer when God questioned her and Adam in the garden? Why do we often do the same thing?

Sometimes as Christians we tend to think we shouldn't be struggling, so we suppress our sin. Or we fear what others will think if they see our sin, so we pretend it's not there or try to cover it up. Other times, we are not even aware of our sin, which should signal to us that we are not centering our lives on God. If we were, our condition before him would be more on the forefront of our minds.

In what ways do you live as if you are god and everything is centered on you? Why do believers frequently not see their idol worship as the sin it is?

How does seeing the extent of your sin as beyond bad external behavior enlarge your understanding of Jesus as your mediator?

Seeing how Moses pleaded with God to be gracious with the Israelites even when their sin offended him puts into perspective what Jesus did for us. So, though we don't like to see our sin, it is actually a good thing as it shows us more of our need and leads us to greater adoration and praise of Jesus.

11

EXERCISE

FACING OUR FALSE GODS

15 minutes

This exercise will help you examine your heart by looking at your own golden calves and what drives them. Spend five to ten minutes following the given prompts. When you've finished, you'll have a chance to share some of what you've discovered.

1. Use the blank space within the illustrated calf, or some notepaper, to list one or more of your false gods that come to mind. For example, if it's very important to you to win acceptance and approval from your friends, write *acceptance from friends*. If nothing readily comes to mind, spend a moment in prayer asking God to show you your sin.
2. Now write down something you tend to do because of that false god. For example: *I post whatever I think will make me look good to my friends and will get me "likes" and comments.*

3. Take this process one step further. This time try to explain why you turn to your false god. For example: *I want to be accepted by my friends because it makes me feel like I have worth and am loved.*

Now if you are willing, share with the group some of what you wrote down.

Why do you think it might be helpful to see both how and why you turn to your false gods?

WRAP-UP AND PRAYER *5 minutes*

Tracing your sin and identifying idols is a lifelong process. It helps to see the root of your sin so you can repent fully. Do it not in a shameful, beat-yourself-up way, but in a way that stirs up a deeper adoration for Jesus being the mediator who saved you from all your sin.

As part of your prayer time, thank God for sending Jesus so that you can have a relationship with God that's free of fear or condemnation.

12

FACE OF GOD

BIG IDEA

God is both just and merciful, but his presence and grace shine upon us through Christ.

BIBLE CONVERSATION *20 minutes*

We have been on a long journey with the Israelites and have come to our last lesson in Exodus. It is a few chapters before the end of the book, but we have already looked at those in our lesson on the tabernacle. To set the stage for today's reading, remember Moses had come down to the base of Mount Sinai to deal with the people after the golden calf incident. We don't know what plague God sent as a consequence of their false worship, but the fact that he did leaves us with the overriding question of today's lesson: Does our sin threaten to keep God's presence from dwelling with us?

What do you think? Does our sin jeopardize God's presence with us? Why or why not?

Take turns reading aloud these passages from Exodus 33 and 34.

Exodus 33:1–3

Exodus 33:12–23

Exodus 34:1–10

Exodus 34:27–33

Throughout Exodus we've seen God's faithful, steadfast love to the Israelites. Even though God is full of grace and mercy, he is also holy and just and cannot simply ignore sin. God's people realized this deeply when, as a consequence of their idolatry, God sent an angel with them instead of personally dwelling in their midst as he had been doing. So while his love for the people was not removed, their sin caused a separation.

How have you seen this similar tension play out in your relationship with your parents? Or maybe in knowing how your church handles church discipline? Or perhaps in a situation of tough love where justice and mercy have both been at play?

Before you move to the article, why do you think God told Moses no one could see his face?

✳✳✳✳

Today's article will shed light on the question of why no one was able to see God's face. Take turns as you read it aloud.

ARTICLE

FULL IN HIS
WONDERFUL FACE

5 minutes

Emily was at school when she got this text from her dad: "I know what you are up to." That was all it said, but it was enough to make her start freaking out. What exactly did he know? And how did he know? For the rest of the day she was consumed by it and dreaded going home to face him.

When the final bell rang, she delayed going home as long as she could. But since her dad worked from home, she knew he would be expecting her. What would he say? Would he buy her story? Could she really fool him? If not, she knew she would have to kiss her social life goodbye for who knows how long.

But after sitting in her parked car for a few minutes, she decided to just tell the truth, knowing it always turns out better that way. She slowly opened the back door and walked into the kitchen. He always heard her come in, and if he wasn't on the phone, he came to greet her and sit while she had a snack. But that wasn't the case today.

She could hear him rustling in his office, not on the phone. Surely, he knew she was home. Should she go in there to face him? All day she had dreaded seeing him, but now his lack of acknowledgment made the anticipation of his anger even worse.

But then the unexpected happened: he came around the corner and, to her shock, reached out his arms and pulled her near. Their talk followed and consequences were handed down, but in that first moment, she got what she needed most—confirmation of his unending love.

Do you recall a time you've needed affirmation of your parent's unconditional love as Emily did? What about with God? Has your sin ever kept you in a place of feeling as though God had or would remove his love from you?

When Emily's dad moved toward her and embraced her, she knew it would all be okay. Yes, she still got in trouble, but her sinful behavior did not cause her dad to reject her. His look of love was what she needed most.

That's what Moses needed, too. After God sent a plague and then told Moses he would not go with them to the Promised Land, Moses feared the sins of the people had been too much this time. Sure, the substitute angel might guarantee military, political, and economic success. But as far as Moses was concerned, without God accompanying them life was pointless and they might as well die.

In our culture we don't tend to think this way. For us, life is not found in God. But we do like all of the benefits and blessings of God. So to most of us, God's offer to Moses requiring no sacrifice, upkeep, or relation-ship, while still granting full protection and success, sounds awesome. But what we fail to realize is that the gnawing emptiness and never-ending search for approval, acceptance, and acclaim would remain. This is because true life and satisfaction can't be found in anything except God's acceptance—his look of love, his face!

Moses understood this, which is why he pleaded, "Please show me your glory." Or, to say it another way, "Let me have your face!" *Glory* and *face* are synonymous here. In addition to *glory*, the Hebrew word *panim* used in chapters 33 and 34 for *presence* means "face." So when

God said, "My presence will not go with you," it was his face—his full acceptance—he was withholding from the people.

To that end, in answer to the question posed earlier, all sin (no matter how big or small) does jeopardize God's presence with us. Because of sin, we can't have the one thing we need. We can't see God's face. That is, unless God chooses mercy.

This brings us back to the basic truth of God's sovereignty. This is crucial to making sense of a God who is so holy he cannot tolerate sin but at the same time loves to give grace to the guilty. Apart from ruling over all things and therefore being free to act according to who *he* is, we would have no hope of seeing his face and knowing his loving acceptance. In other words, if his actions in any way depended on *us*, then he would be obligated to give us what we deserve. And if we deserve his wrath and justice because of our sin, this is what we would receive.

The weight of this tension was felt by Moses: "You say to me, 'Bring up this people,' but you have not let me know whom you will send with me" (Exodus 33:12). What he was really asking was, "What name will go with us? Will it be justice or mercy?"

But Moses had forgotten the name God revealed back at the burning bush. If you recall, *I AM WHO I AM* was God's proclamation of his absolute sovereignty. It's the same name he gave again when he said, "I will make all my goodness pass before you and will proclaim before you my name 'The LORD.' And I will be gracious to whom I will be gracious, and will show mercy on whom I will show mercy" (Exodus 33:19).

It was as if God said, "Moses, the essence of who I am is not either/or, it's both. I am presently and eternally both merciful *and* just."

Hearing this didn't relieve the tension for Moses; he wanted to see it to believe it. Therefore, God took him up to a cleft in the rock so Moses could see all of his goodness pass by. And while Moses saw it, it wasn't God's face, only his back. Still, when he came off the mountain, his face was shining and the people noticed it and were afraid to come near him. Something was different about him. He was changed by the display of God's glory.

Moses did not get God's face because only later at the cross would the full radiance of God's glory be displayed in the face of another man who got God's back. But this time God turned his back toward his own Son who would bear the severity of the Father's justice and wrath so you and I could look full into his wonderful face. And how beautiful is that face?

Like Moses, it is in seeing his goodness to us that we are being transformed. But unlike Moses who had to cover his face, "we all, with unveiled face, beholding the glory of the Lord" (2 Corinthians 3:18) can see the glory of God through his Son. "For God, who said, 'Let light shine out of darkness,' has shone in our hearts to give the light of the knowledge of the glory of God in the face of Jesus Christ." (4:6).

DISCUSSION *10 minutes*

Like Emily, we all crave affirmation—especially from a parent, after we've sinned or felt as if we've disappointed them. But the deeper question is how has your sin affected your relationship with God? Have you feared his rejection? If so, did it cause you to try to make amends or lead you to run from him? How did that work for you?

Moses too needed to know God's presence would still be with them. Life without God was not worth living, even with his tangible benefits through the angel.

What do you think is the difference between having God's presence and eternal favor versus earthly benefits?

Someone who only wants God's blessings and benefits and not a relationship with him does not truly understand God. As we've talked about, God desires a personal relationship with us. That was why he wanted the tabernacle built so he could dwell with his people. It is why he calls *us* to his Word, to be in church and into fellowship with other believers. But to seek after only his blessing exposes a false belief that our behavior, or misbehavior, is what influences God's blessing or withholding of blessing.

This is not to say our behavior doesn't matter. Our sin does jeopardize God's presence, but for those who look to Jesus as Yahweh we receive all of his goodness as our covering and guarantee of God's steadfast, loyal love to us even when we sin.

Since this is true, and we see Moses's transformation came through beholding God's glory, why do we focus our Bible reading so much on how to apply it to our lives rather than how it reveals God's glory in Christ?

HEADS OR TAILS?

15 minutes

Take out a coin if you have one, or get one from your leader or a friend. Hold it in your hand. You can see it has both a heads side and a tails side. But even though each side is different, it is still just one coin. You can't have a front without a back. Without both sides, it would not be a coin.

This is how it is with God. He is a God of both justice and mercy at the same time. He can't be only one or the other. So, though we may want to flip the coin and always get heads (his face), the tails side of our holy God—how he demands justice and abhors sin—is part of his glory. And that makes the mercy, love, and grace he extends to his children all the greater.

Use the next few minutes to journal what you have learned about God from his description of himself in this chapter. How does this personally affect you?

that God does choose grace & the
fact that He does rather then
turning away from me shows His
eternal love for us.

_____

_____

_____

_____

_____

_____

_____

If you really lived believing you are more sinful than you realized but more deeply loved by God than you can imagine, how might it cause you to shine as Moses did when he came down off the mountain after having seen God's goodness?

For example, do you think it would affect your demeanor or stance toward God? Toward others? How might it affect your view of yourself? Your relationships?

you would radadbt God's presence bc
of being filled w/ it yourself.
you know what God has done for
us & you are so thankfull that
you want to be like Him.

_____

_____

_____

_____

_____

_____

_____

When you finish, share with the group some of what you wrote from the questions above.

If someone asked you what the book of Exodus is about, what would you tell them? How would you show them it points to Jesus? What would you say is the greatest thing you learned from Exodus?

WRAP-UP AND PRAYER *5 minutes*

The end of this study does not mean you are done digging into God's Word. Keep studying the Bible, for in it you will see God's face and be transformed. As a part of your prayer time, ask God to help you fix your eyes on his face. Ask that his light would shine through you.

LEADER'S NOTES

LESSON 1: FORGETFUL OR FAITHFUL?

Bible Conversation. This first lesson looks at Israel's slavery in Exodus 1 and 2. Included in Exodus 2 is the beginning of Moses's life. As a central figure to the book of Exodus, it is important he be included and discussed here, although he is not the primary focus of the lesson.

Article. The article will help the reader grasp the big idea of the text and of this week's lesson: God never leaves us stranded—left to face our circumstances, situations, or sin alone. Depending on where the conversations about the article lead, you might want to reach out privately to those who may still be struggling to believe God is faithful despite hard times.

Exercise. The point of the exercise is to consider the depth of our own enslavement. While the Israelites found themselves in the wrong place and under the wrong rule, we, too, live enslaved under the wrong ruler. But there was One who never succumbed to sin so he could set us free from its bondage.

LESSON 2: THE GREAT I AM

Extra materials needed: Dry erase board or flip chart

Bible Conversation. This lesson's Bible passage starts with God revealing himself to Moses out of the burning bush. In the conversation that ensues, we learn God wants Moses to lead the Israelite people out of Egypt. As you read and discuss, make it your goal to help participants see what we can know about God as the great I AM, and why he is worthy of Moses's faith—and ours.

If you have access to a dry erase board or flip chart, it may be helpful to write out participants' observations during the Bible Conversation. During the Bible reading, the group will be asked to note four responses Moses had to God. Those four responses were:

1.   Who am I? Why should I be the one to go?
2.   Who are you? What shall I say is your name?
3.   What if the people don't believe me?
4.   I am not eloquent.

Article. The article explains the big idea of the text and of this week's lesson: what we can know about God as the great I AM who promises to be present with us, and why he is worthy of Moses's faith, and ours.

Exercise. The exercise will help participants see who God is for them as the great I AM in specific, personal ways. Encourage them to fill out the chart in their books or write down their responses on notepaper. If participants don't seem ready to share what they've written, be prepared to share your own struggles.

OUTSIDE READING: Assign participants to read Exodus 5 through 12:32 on their own, and to underline or make notes about what stands out to them, prior to the next meeting.

LESSON 3: PLAGUED

Bible Conversation. Over and over again Moses and Aaron ask Pharaoh to let God's people go. As a power struggle plays out, Pharaoh continues to harden despite the devastating effects of the plagues. Multiple themes will be brought into this lesson, but the overriding issue to be presented is that God is the one true king who is all-powerful, over all things, and as merciful as he is just.

Article. The article aims to show participants, through the plagues, that God controls the forces of nature and also restores order to chaos.

And while God is a Judge, his purpose in the plagues is not to destroy but to save.

Exercise. The purpose of the exercise is to show that by trying to order our lives and control our circumstances, we end up like Pharaoh. We live as if we are our own god. To complete the exercise, participants will need to write in their books or on notepaper.

LESSON 4: THE TRUE SACRIFICE

Bible Conversation. This lesson looks at the tenth plague, the death of the firstborn, to understand its significance and how it ties to the institution of Passover. The goal is for participants to see the Passover lamb as a pointer to Jesus, who is the ultimate sacrifice.

Article. The article will help participants see how the final plague, the significance of the firstborn, and the Israelites' exodus out of Egypt represent our story of redemption through Jesus.

Exercise. The goal of the exercise is to see Christ as the true Passover Lamb. Participants will need to write their answers in the book or on notepaper. The Scripture passages in the exercise match the lamb titles in the following order:

The Lamb who covers our shame
The Provided Lamb
The Passover Lamb
The Unblemished Lamb
The Lamb wounded for us
The coming Lamb who removes sin
The Lamb who is Jesus
The ransoming Lamb
The reigning Lamb

LESSON 5: FREEDOM

Bible Conversation. Today's text is the account of the Israelites crossing through the Red Sea to safety. For the first time in more than four hundred years they are free! Participants will look at how this foreshadows our salvation and what it tells us about God's faithfulness to deliver.

NOTE: Use the opening icebreaker question in the Bible Conversation, about stress and fear, to help participants see that a lack of control or a lack of trust in God is often the root cause underneath our stress, anxiety, and fear. Be prepared to share your own example.

Article. The Red Sea crossing is a picture of our salvation. In the article we will see how God alone worked to deliver the Israelites. In the same way, it is God alone who works to bring us to a saving knowledge of him, and God alone who works to keep us (sanctify us) until completion.

NOTE: The final discussion question after the article asks how the Red Sea is a pattern for our salvation. If necessary, help participants to see that God alone is the initiator and sustainer of our salvation. This means he not only does all the work necessary to save us, but he will do everything needed to keep us secure in his grip for the remainder of our lives. For Biblical reference, see (and or read aloud with students) the following verses: Psalm 70:12–16; John 6:65; 10:27–29; Romans 8:30; 1 Corinthians 1:30–31; Ephesians 1:3–14; 2:8–10; Philippians 1:6.

Exercise. For the exercise, the participants will answer some questions on their own before sharing together. They may want to write out their answers.

LESSON 6: BREAD OF LIFE

Bible Conversation. This lesson picks up the Israelites' story after they crossed the Red Sea into the wilderness. It won't take long before they doubt Moses's and God's goodness again, even though God faithfully provides them with manna as their daily bread.

Article. The article will help readers see how Jesus is the true manna—the Bread of Life and our sustainer.

NOTE: The final discussion question after the article asks about God's faithfulness, described in Lamentations 3:22–24. If necessary, help participants see that despite the Israelites' grumbling and failure to follow instructions, God never stopped providing for and sustaining them. This is who God is for us, too. He does not want us to run, hide, or try to fix ourselves. But this is what we so often do when we have sinned, or when we think we have failed him because we haven't been faithful. It is exactly why God gave us his Son as the bread of heaven—his perfect provision for sin because of his love for us.

Exercise. Give the group enough time to consider the questions and jot down some notes if they want to, before going back through the questions together.

LESSON 7: WATER FROM THE ROCK

Bible Conversation. The Bible Conversation is intended to show how the behavior of the Israelites in the wilderness should not surprise us. Neither, however, should God's gracious response.

Article. The article explains how Jesus is the true Rock who received the judgment we deserve. Because he did, we have the full assurance of the ultimate covenant, sealed by his death—that he is with us always.

Exercise. The point of the exercise is to provide Scripture to reorient us from grumbling self-talk to seeing Jesus as our rock! Participants will need to write in their books or have pen and paper available for brief notes.

LESSON 8: COVENANT CONFIRMED

Bible Conversation. The primary purpose of today's lesson is to see why God gives his Law as the confirmation of his covenant to his people.

Article. The article will help the reader see God as the initiator and keeper of his covenant to his people, and also see that his Law was given as a sign of his love for his people.

Exercise. The point of the exercise is to see God's dual nature. He is a holy God to be greatly feared, but also a personal, loving God who desires our relationship.

LESSON 9: THE LAW DECONSTRUCTED

Bible Conversation. We tend to look at the Ten Commandments with a legalistic understanding and think we are doing well because we haven't murdered someone. But as the lesson develops, participants will see that if we have ever even been angry at someone we have murdered them in our hearts. Oh, how much more we need Jesus than we care to see! This is the point of today's lesson—for the Ten Commandments to expose the participants to the true condition of their hearts.

NOTE: In the Bible Conversation, participants are asked to divide the Ten Commandments under two headings. Commandments one to four fall under *love your God*, and commandments five through ten under *love your neighbor*. Participants are also asked about the heart behind the commandments. The heart that disobeys the command to *"have no other gods before me"* is idolatrous. And failing to love your neighbor as yourself means allowing something other than God to rule your heart, likely your own self.

Article. The article will help the reader better understand what each commandment requires, and how we constantly fall short. Seeing our imperfection is one of the purposes of the Law. But the goal in recognizing our true condition is for participants to see who Christ is for us as the only one who could perfectly keep God's command.

NOTE: During this discussion, help participants see that when we look at the commandments with a legalistic view, we wrongly think we are doing pretty well and don't see how much we need Jesus.

Exercise. This exercise leads participants to reflect on specific ways we all fall short of each commandment, with the goal of opening eyes to the reality of our extreme need of Christ's grace and perfection. Encourage participants to jot down their responses in their books or on notepaper.

OUTSIDE READING: Assign participants to read Exodus chapters 25 through 31 prior to the next meeting and be ready to discuss it.

LESSON 10: TABERNACLE

Bible Conversation. This lesson is a flyover study of the tabernacle. With so many chapters, only enough Scripture to formulate the main idea will be read out loud. The goal is for the participants to see that God wants to dwell with his people. For the Israelites, God's presence was with them through the tabernacle. This is because they couldn't see him face-to-face or have direct interaction with him. But through the tabernacle we see a picture of God's centrality to all of life that we now know more fully in Christ.

NOTE: If the participants need a hint during the Bible Conversation, share that serving others, being aware of the needs of others, encouraging someone, being disciplined, restraining from sin could all be called acts of worship.

Article. The article explains the purpose behind God's elaborate instructions and design for the tabernacle. The participants will come to see how it sets a pattern for making our worship of God central to all of our life. Additionally, Jesus will be revealed to be the true tabernacle. Upon his death, the veil in the temple was torn because we would no longer need a priest to serve as our mediator. Jesus was the perfect high priest, once and for all.

Exercise. In the exercise, the tabernacle diagram will provide a better visual for the details brought out in the article. The exercise will walk participants through each item to see how Christ has fulfilled its purpose perfectly. They will need to write in their books or on notepaper to complete this exercise. Answers to the fill in the blanks are listed in order as the questions occur: *courtyard gate, washing basin, priest, lampstand, table of showbread, bronze altar of sacrifice,* and *gold altar of incense.*

LESSON 11: A GOLDEN IDOL

Bible Conversation. In reading Exodus 32, participants will see how quickly we turn away from the God we say we love to the false gods we think will give us what we want. God's anger over sin is apparent in this chapter, but we will see how Moses is the precursor to Christ, our mediator, who took on God's wrath once and for all to ensure our right standing before him as his chosen people.

NOTE: In modern terms, "*eat, drink and rose up to play*" means the festival included getting drunk and engaging in uninhibited sexual sin. God saying, "Go down to *your* people . . ." might be like a mother saying to her husband, "You should've seen what *your* son did . . ." It doesn't mean she doesn't love her son anymore, but she is angry with him. Likewise, by God referring to his covenant children only as Moses's people, he is not removing his love from them, but he is angry!

Article. The article will help participants see Moses as a pointer to Jesus, who is our true and perfect mediator.

Exercise. The point of the exercise is for participants to see their false gods, not so that they beat themselves up, but instead so that they can gain a deeper adoration of what Jesus did for them. Encourage them to write out their responses.

LESSON 12: FACE OF GOD

Extra materials needed: A coin for each participant to hold

Bible Conversation. This lesson explores how God is equally just and merciful at the same time as well as why his sovereignty is crucial to receiving grace instead of what we deserve. The initial conversation and Bible reading will prepare participants for the crux of the lesson, which will be more fully revealed in the article and exercise.

Article. The article expounds on the scriptures by showing Moses again as a pointer to Christ. Though Moses was shown all of God's goodness, he could not see God's face. But since the better Moses, Christ, also had God's back turned to him when he was forsaken on the cross, we can now look full into God's face to receive all of his goodness, glory, and grace.

Exercise. The point of the exercise is to help the participants see that God's justice cannot be separated from his character, and that actually it is because of his holy, righteous standard that the grace and mercy he extends to us is all the more beautiful. This exercise requires writing in the books or on notepaper.

ACKNOWLEDGMENTS

Apart from my husband, this book (as with the other two) would not be possible. Pete, your long-ago Exodus sermon series, along with your continued faithful preaching and teaching of the gospel and the extra hours you have given to my writing, are the backbone to this book. I love you and am thankful for all that you do for me and our family. And to you, Rebecca, David, and Jonathan—for all the days my writing has taken precedence over you, thank you for extending me grace and supporting me unconditionally.

To my friend Cheryl Devoe, thank you for working through another manuscript with yet the same grammatical errors. You would think I would have learned by now, but it seems no matter how many times you correct *then* and *than*, *affect* and *effect*, and the countless misplaced or missing commas, I still get it wrong!

And to Barbara Juliani, Cheryl White, Gretchen Logterman, Ruth Castle, Jack Klumpenhower and the rest of the New Growth Press team, I'm so thankful for the role each of you have played in taking my books from start to finish. I could not ask for a better publishing team. Above all, I am thankful that New Growth Press saw the need for a book of Bible studies for teens and has an unwavering commitment to gospel-centered books on the whole. Included in this is also Serge, for their partnership with New Growth Press to get gospel resources into the hands of students.

mission
propelled by good news

At Serge we believe that mission begins through the gospel of Jesus Christ bringing God's grace into the lives of believers. This good news also sustains and empowers us to cross nations and cultures to bring the gospel of grace to those whom God is calling to himself.

As a cross-denominational, reformed, sending agency with more than 200 missionaries and 25 teams in 5 continents, we are always looking for people who are ready to take the next step in sharing Christ, through:

- **Short-term Teams**: One- to two-week trips oriented around serving overseas ministries while equipping the local church for mission
- **Internships:** Eight-week to nine-month opportunities to learn about missions through serving with our overseas ministry teams
- **Apprenticeships:** Intensive 12–24 month training and ministry opportunities for those discerning their call to cross-cultural ministry
- **Career:** One- to five-year appointments designed to nurture you for a lifetime of ministry

 Grace at the Fray   **Visit us online at: serge.org/mission**

spiritual renewal resources for you

Disciples who are motivated and empowered by grace to reach out to a broken world are handmade, not mass-produced. Serge intentionally grows disciples through curriculum, discipleship experiences, and training programs.

Resources for Every Stage of Growth

Serge offers grace-based, gospel-centered studies for every stage of the Christian journey. Every level of our materials focuses on essential aspects of how the Spirit transforms and motivates us through the gospel of Jesus Christ.

- **101**: The Gospel-Centered Series
  Gospel-centered studies on Christian growth, community, work, parenting, and more.

- **201**: The Gospel Transformation Series
  These studies go a step deeper into gospel transformation, involve homework and more in-depth Bible study

- **301**: The Sonship Course and Serge Individual Mentoring

Mentored Sonship

For more than 25 years Serge has been discipling ministry leaders around the world through our Sonship course to help them experience the freedom and joy of having the gospel transform every part of their lives. A personal discipler will help you apply what you are learning to the daily struggles and situations you face, as well as, model what a gospel-centered faith looks and feels like.

Discipler Training Course

Serge's Discipler Training Course helps you gain biblical understanding and practical wisdom you need to disciple others so they experience substantive, lasting growth in their lives. Available for onsite training or via distance learning, our training programs are ideal for ministry leaders, small group leaders or those seeking to grow in their ability to disciple effectively.

 Grace at the Fray   **Find more resources at serge.org**

resources and mentoring
for every stage of
growth

Every day around the world, Serge teams help people develop and deepen a living, breathing, growing relationship with Jesus. We help people connect with God in ways that are genuinely grace-motivated and increase desire and ability to reach out to others. No matter where you are along the way, we have a series that is right for you.

101: The *Gospel-Centered* Series

Our *Gospel-Centered* series is simple, deep, and transformative. Each *Gospel-Centered* lesson features an easy-to-read article and provides challenging discussion questions and application questions. Best of all, no outside preparation on the part of the participants is needed! They are perfect for small groups, those who are seeking to develop "gospel DNA" in their organizations and leaders, and contexts where people are still wrestling with what it means to follow Jesus.

201: The *Gospel Transformation* Series

Our *Gospel Transformation* studies take the themes introduced in our 101-level materials and expand and deepen them. Designed for those seeking to grow through directly studying Scripture each *Gospel Transformation* lesson helps participants grow in the way they understand and experience God's grace. Ideal for small groups, individuals who are ready for more, and one-on-one mentoring, *Gospel Identity, Gospel Growth,* and *Gospel Love* provide substantive material, in easy-to-use, manageable sized studies.

The *Sonship* Course and Individual Mentoring from Serge

Developed for use with our own missionaries and used for over 25 years with thousands of Christian leaders in every corner of the world, Sonship sets the standard for whole-person, life transformation through the gospel. Designed to be used with a mentor, or in groups ready for a high investment with each other, each lesson focuses on the type of "inductive heart study" that brings about change from the inside out.

 Grace at the Fray   **Visit us online at serge.org**